Come, Let Us Pray!

by

Dr. J. Emmette Weir

PNEUMA LIFE

PUBLISHING

COME, LET US PRAY!

by J. Emmette Weir

Published by:

PUBLISHING

Printed in the United States of America
Copyright © 1993 - J. Emmette Weir

Come Let Us Pray ISBN 1-56229-202-1

Pneuma Life Publishing
P.O. Box 10612
Bakersfield, CA 93389
(805) 837-2113 Phone
(805) 837-0302 FAX

Contents

Acknowledgements

The apostle Paul, writing to the small Christian community at Corinth, put the challenging, thought provoking question, "What do ye have, which ye have not received?" Here we are reminded, through this letter to these Christians, written nearly two thousand years ago, of the profound truth that in all that we achieve in our sojourn through this transitory life, we are greatly indebted to others! This is certainly true of this work, which would not have been possible without the encouragement, support and labors of many persons, whom the Lord has used, sometimes in most unexpected ways, to help me in the production of this book.

I would, therefore, like to take this opportunity to express my deep sense of gratitude to: "The Faithful Few" members of Ebenezer Methodist Church, East Shirley Street, Nassau, Bahamas, who attended the Prayer Meetings on Tuesday evenings and "foreday" on Thursdays, whose spiritual endeavors, first inspired me to begin work on a book on prayer,. while ministering there (1981-1986). Mr. Alfred Stewart, dynamic Christian layman, prominent Bahamian Banker and organizer of the Bahamas National Call to Prayer 1991- 1992, who greatly encouraged me in preparing the material for this book. Mrs. Ava Forber and Mrs. Lynn Armstrong, secretaries at Templeton Theological Seminary, who, with unfailing patience and consummate skill, transformed my poorly executed typescript into a neat, legible product. Mrs. Earthel L. Smith, who working with deft skill and a smile, committed it to a wordprocessor. Mr. Wellington Chea, who did the editing and also Sir Leonard Knowles, Mr. Oswald Munnings and Mrs. Lily Weir-Coakley, Librarian, who assisted in Proof Reading. Mr. Bertram Knowles, Captain Durward "Sea Wolf" Knowles and Mrs. Dianne M. Kemp for encouragement and practical assistance. The Rev. Wilbert Forker, Chairman, Board of Trustees, Templeton Theological Seminary, a school of theology in the commonwealth of the Bahamas. Sir John Templeton, Moving spirit behind the prestigious Templeton Prize for Progress in Religion and Templeton Theological Seminary.

Dr. Myles Munroe, President of Bahamas Faith Ministries. Dr Kevin Alcena, President Alcena credit International Corporation and The McHari Institute, an International Educational Foundation based in Nassau, Bahamas. Evangelist Rex Major, the Rev. Dr. Fr. Patrick Pinder, The Rev. Dr. Charles Smith and the Ven. Archdeacon William Thompson, all Clergymen serving in the Bahamas and Mrs. Genevieve Luna, Assistant Librarian, The Stitt Library, Austin Presbterian Theological Seminary, Austin, Texas, for their kind assistance in compiling the list of additional resources for the development of one's prayer life. Ena, My dear faithful wife, Ellsworth and Erica, who, though not complaining, just wondered why "Daddy was typing so much!". To God be the glory, great things He hath done!

Dedication

In Loving Memory of:
Eunice Jeanette Weir
1910–1965
Great teacher
Great Mother
Great Christian
and Sister Zoe Knowles
"A Great Woman of Prayer"

...and to:
My Dear Loving Father
Gaspar Emmett Weir

...and to:
The many "Prayer Warriors" participants in
The Bahamas National Call To Prayer
1991–1992

Foreword

The subject of prayer is one of the oldest and most inexhaustible topics explored throughout the ages and yet today it is still one of the dearest and most written about of all subjects.

From the earliest records of civilization, man has always sought to touch the unknown and has aspired to achieve a relationship and communication with a higher being. Some have addressed their prayer to the elements of creation, such as the sun, the moon, the stars, nature, animals and the beasts of the ocean. Others have attempted to tap into the spirit world through different mediums, all under the guise of some big form of prayer.

However, the biblical context in which prayer is recorded is very clear and yet so complex that the Bible expresses a multiplicity of approaches to this subject . There are also many different types of prayer recorded in Scripture and but they are all made to the one and same God Jehovah. This intimate and very vital part of the Christian faith is one of the foundational elements entrenched in the heart of the development of the individual's walk with God.

In the volume "Come Let Us Pray" Dr. Emmette Weir has once again added to the wealth of knowledge and information on this subject. This document is not just an academic exercise or a theological exposition on the topic but is the outgrowth of a personal relationship and commitment and experience during a crucial period in the life of this nation, The Bahamas, during which time the entire nation was called to prayer, in which Dr. Weir played an active part in the national organization of this national event.

The principles and concepts recorded in this book can also be used to assist any other individual in capturing the heart and the spirit of the intercessor for the national life of his nation and community.

I highly recommend and commend the document to all of those who desire to enhance their prayer life and to learn how to activate an mobilize others to do the same. I trust that you will enjoy the material therein and find a maturing effect on your own personal development.

- Dr. Myles Munroe
Bahamas Faith Ministries

Introduction

"Lord, teach us to pray as John also taught his disciples" (Luke 11:1). The disciples of Jesus came to Him with this simple request. These disciples, who had spent much time with the Master, and most certainly had witnessed Him often at prayer, wanted Him to teach them to pray.

It is noteworthy that they did not request Him to teach them to preach, or to do pastoral visitation, or even to heal, though it is recorded that there were times when they experienced difficulty in exercising the healing ministry (Mark 9:14-19), Cf. Matt. 17:14-21, Luke 9:37-45). They specifically asked Him to teach them to pray!

There is something very significant here. For, that they requested Him to give them lessons in prayer indicated that they thought that such instruction was essential. Why did the disciples ask the Master to teach them to pray?

When we reflect deeply upon the nature and meaning of prayer, it is not at all difficulty to understand the reason for this request. Prayer is at once very simple and most profound. "Prayer is the soul's sincere desire uttered or unexpressed."

Thus one of the great hymn writers of the Church describes prayer. There is much for us to think about in this definition of prayer: for it is essentially a deeply spiritual matter. Prayer is at the heart of mankind's spiritual quest.

Prayer is, in one sense, very simple. Even a small child can pray to God. Indeed, sometimes we are amazed at the spiritual insight which children display in their prayer, especially at bedtime.

But, on the other hand, it is a tremendous spiritual exercise, which requires years of practice. Even the most deeply spiritual and seasoned of Christians will confess that they still have much to learn about prayer. Indeed, it is impossible to describe or understand prayer adequately. All we know is that in prayer we are drawn very near to God, and almost instinctively, we bring our concerns to our God.

Since prayer is so simple that even a little child can do so, but so profound that even the most experienced of Christians cannot plumb its spiritual depths, there can be no doubt that it is essential for us to do everything that we possibly can to improve the quality of our prayer life. In other words, PRAYER CAN BE LEARNED. By practice we can improve our prayer life and, therefore, our spiritual walk with God.

Our purpose in this book is to explore the various aspects of prayer with a view to improving the quality of our prayer life - we shall do this by looking first at the main elements of prayer - Praise, Thanksgiving, Petition, Confession and Intercession. We shall also discuss the way in which we should respond when we come up against problems in our prayer life. We shall explore the nature of prayer in terms of listening. Finally, we shall discuss some practical hints which may be applied in this effort to improve our prayer life.

Properly used, this book should contribute greatly to enriching the spiritual development of the reader.

1

*W*HAT *I*S *P*RAYER?

If you were to ask a group (any group) of people, "What is prayer?" you would probably get as many answers as persons in the group; for prayer can be defined in many different ways. For instance, the following are some of the definitions of prayer given by the participants in a session on prayer:

> Prayer is a family conversing with God.
> Prayer is saying, "I'm sorry" to God and asking for grace not to repeat our failure.
> Prayer is a child's simplest form of communication with God.
> Prayer is talking to God.
> Prayer is bringing to God my deep concern for those who are near to me, my family and my close circle of friends.
> Prayer is the way to inner peace.
> "And the prayer of faith shall save the sick."
> Prayer is laying before God a concern for our enemies.
> Prayer is work.
> Prayer is where our hopes are confirmed, faith is enriched.
> Prayer is a deep unuttered desire within a human heart.

As we examine these varied definitions of prayer, reflect upon others we have heard or seen elsewhere. Most significantly, think about our own definition, can we discern a common idea linking them, in some way, with one another? Is there a recurring theme which emerges as the meaning of prayer is examined in depth? The answer - communion with God!

Yes, it may be confidently asserted that prayer is, first and foremost, communion with God. Or, as "metropolitan anthony", with typical vigor, precision and spiritual insight, puts it:

Prayer is primarily an encounter with God. On certain occasions we may be aware of God's presence, more often dimly so, but there are times when we can place ourselves before Him only by an act of faith, without being aware of His presence at all. It is not the degree of our awareness that is relevant, that makes this encounter possible and fruitful; other conditions must be fulfilled, the basic one being that the person should be real.

In prayer, then, we draw near to God; we seek to enter into an intimate relationship with our Maker. In prayer, we humbly approach God expressing our inmost and most cherished thoughts, secrets which we dare to reveal only to our nearest and dearest of human associates. The Psalmist expresses it very well in the immortal words:

"Trust   in him at all times; ye people, pour out your heart before him: God is a refuge for us" (Psalms   662::8).

Conversely, in prayer, God draws near to us. As such, it is the supreme form of communion between God and man. For, in prayer, God comes to meet us where we are. He graciously condescends to dwell with us as we aspire to meet Him.

Prayer is utterly essential for spiritual growth. John Wesley, a giant of the devotional life, who arose every morning at four to pray, often urged his fellow Christians, *"Do not neglect the means of grace!"* Among these means of grace, prayer occupies a place of prime importance.   It is written "We perish if we cease from prayer." This is indeed the case. Spiritually, we do perish when we neglect prayer; for we lack nourishment for our souls. This is why St. Paul exhorts us in I Thess. 5:17 to *"Pray without ceasing!"*

Prayer, then, is an intensely spiritual experience! Prayer is natural, it is "second nature" to man because man is a spiritual being. This is what is meant in the Bible when it is stated that "God breathed into man the breath of life and man became a living soul." (Genesis 2:7). It is this living soul, this spiritual aspect of man which is nourished in communion with God. Prayer is the chief means of this spiritual nourishment. In a sense most profound, it may be claimed that prayer is to the soul what breathing is to the body - the means by which it is sustained. Yes, prayer is essential for the nurture of the soul.

Thus, if you were to ask a deeply spiritual person, a saint of the Church who is committed to a life of prayer, why he/she devotes so much time to prayer, the answer would simply be, "I can't help it! " Prayer is so natural for the true Christian that he does not have to learn it. Yet, in a deeper sense, he or she still has to keep learning more about prayer for life, so that it may continue to be a source of spiritual growth and strength. In prayer, earnest prayer, we are strengthened as we wait upon the Lord.

Thus the prophet Isaiah declares:

"....They that wait upon the LORD shall renew their strength; they shall mount up with wings as eagles; they shall run, and not be weary; they shall walk, and not faint" (Isaiah 40:31).

There is no greater source of spiritual power than prayer! For it draws us into a deep, abiding and refreshing communion with our God. Words, mere words, cannot adequately express the depth of our spiritual joy, the height of our ecstasy as we dwell continually in the Divine Presence...in prayer. How profound our joy, how elevated our spirits when we commune with the LORD as "friend to friend." Yes, it is true that we really do bear much needless pain and sorrow when we do not allow the Spirit of God to envelop us in prayer! Thus it is our duty, our great privilege to seek constantly the Divine Presence in prayer. There is no sweeter communion than that which we experience in deep and earnest prayer.

Thus, because the experience of prayer is so intensely personal, no two persons can have precisely the same experience. Rather, each and everyone has to come to his/her understanding in the context of a personal encounter with the Living God. This is precisely why we cannot really describe the experience of prayer to anyone else. In the final analysis, the best we can do, is to testify to them of the great benefits that we have received as a result of our prayer.

Yes, we can join with the Psalmist in inviting them:

> "Oh taste and see that the LORD is good" *(Psalm 34:8)* .

Therefore, we must *take time to pray*. It is essential, then that we find time to retire from the daily round of our duties and the pressures of "making a living" to be with the LORD. (How easy it is for us to become so obsessed with "making a living" that we devote so very little "to making life worth living!") It is in such moments that we are brought into a deep, satisfying relationship with the Master. In such moments, alone with our Maker, we are refreshed and strengthened to carry out our daily routine with enthusiasm and sincerity, and in a manner which brings glory to Christ. For as we leave the place of earnest prayer, the place of "wrestling with God," like Jacob, we are strengthened to continue our daily endeavors in such a way that we serve with a sense of pride in ourselves, with concern for others, and to the glory of God!

So, my dear friend, let us seek to be continually in communion with the Master by means of prayer! Let us continually abide in the inner chamber, that place "near to the heart of God" where we can truly find rest, recreation and restoration for our weary souls. Let us not be satisfied with "second best." Let us, indeed, dwell continually in the Divine Presence where we shall experience tremendous spiritual growth.

> *"O the pure delight of a single hour*
> *That before Thy throne I spend,*
> *When I kneel in prayer, and with Thee, my God,*
> *I commune as friend with friend.*
> *Draw me nearer, nearer, blessed LORD,*
> *To the Cross where Thou hast died:*
> *Draw me nearer, nearer, nearer, blessed LORD,*
> *To thy precious, bleeding side."*

-**Frances Jean van Alystyne, 1820-1915**

SUMMARY

What can we say about prayer?

1. Prayer is essentially communion with God.

2. Prayer is very simple.

3. Prayer is very profound.

4. Prayer is a means of grace by which, we aspire to reach
    God and God chooses to meet us at our point of need.

5. Prayer is essential for spiritual growth.

2

ℙRAYER 𝐼S ℙRAISE

It was Sunday! The rays of the tropical sun shone brilliantly through the window panes of the main church in a small village located on the north coast of the Caribbean isle. A "hush of expectation" descended upon the large predominantly youthful congregation as it waited for the service to begin. Why such enthusiasm about the service? Because it was to be conducted by the young people of the church, it was Youth Sunday!

The choir, consisting mainly of young people in their teens, dressed in their brightly colored summer uniforms, was seated. Then, as the young preacher ascended the pulpit and announced the Call to Worship:

"Enter His gates with thanksgiving,, and into His courts with praise: be thankful unto him, and bless His name"
    (Psalms 100:4).

The youth choir arose, singing melodiously, burst forth into the well known sacred song of praise:

"Praise Him! Praise Him! Praise Him! Praise Him! "

The choristers were enjoying worship! "Rocking" to the rhythm of the music, they indeed did, "make a joyful noise unto the LORD", as the young organist demonstrated mastery of the keyboard and the other musicians formed a small band playing the drums, guitar and tambourine. They continued signing:

"Praise Him! Praise Him! For He is worthy to be praised! "

The whole congregation, deeply inspired by the singing of the choir, soon joined with its members in praising the Lord, and as

the song ended, they responded with shouts of "Amen!" and
"Praise the Lord!"

Considering the atmosphere which prevailed, there is no
wonder that the congregation joined the choir in singing praise to
the Lord. For the praise of Almighty God is at the very heart of
worship. Indeed, it is the essence of worship. So let us pause for
a moment to consider the meaning of this important aspect of
worship.

Praise, from a deeply spiritual perspective, may best be
described as the human response to the realization of the greatness of God. When we reflected upon the meaning of prayer in the
opening chapter, we saw that it is essentially communion with
God. Very significantly, as we think more deeply about the
meaning of communion with God we come to understand the
nature of praise.

The greatness of God as Creator of all things is profoundly
expressed in the Biblical account of the Creation:

*" In the beginning God created the heavens and the earth. The
earth was without form and void, and darkness was upon the
face of the deep; and the spirit of God was moving over the face
of the waters"'* (Genesis 1:1-2).

As we continue to read and meditate upon this chapter, of the
wonders and mysterious way in which God brought into being the
whole created order, we are moved to acknowledge His greatness
and to proclaim His sustaining grace. Indeed, this theme is
continued throughout the Bible, again and again. The reader is
exhorted to praise God for His wondrous, creative activity and His
sustaining power. That very well known song of praise, "How
Great Thou Art," also illustrates clearly that in the contemplation
of the greatness of God that we are led to offer praise to our Divine
Creator. Indeed, who can meditate truthfully on the greatness of
God as expounded in Holy Scriptures and the hymns of the
Church without bursting forth spontaneously into praises?

Moreover, when we reflect upon the purpose of our existence
as human beings, we are led to appreciate, the meaning of praise.

Again, if we may return to the Creation account, we note that it teaches that mankind has been created in the Divine image. At the pinnacle of the creative process, this principle is declared,

> *"So God created man in His own image, in the image of God He created him; male and female He created them."* (Genesis 1:27, KJV)

This is the basis of the Judaeo-Christian conviction that there is a deep and intimate relationship between God and man, the supreme relationship.

Having been created in the image of God, mankind realizes its true potential in communion with God. Concisely, man is incomplete without God. Or, as Augustine put it:

> *"O Lord, Thou has created us for Thyself and our hearts are restless, until they find their rest in Thee."*

Thus, when we ask the question, "What is the purpose of human existence?" The answer, from the Christian perspective, comes to us in the words of the Westminster Confession:

> *"The true end of man is to worship the LORD and to enjoy Him forever."*

This is just another way of saying that the meaning of human existence is to be found in communion with God. Praise, fundamentally speaking, is the highest activity in which mankind can engage. In praising God, we join with the patriarchs, priests and prophets, with the saints who have passed away and "the saints alive", yes, with all of creation, in acknowledging the Majesty, Holiness and Graciousness of our Creator-God. We praise Him who is revealed in His Divine Son as the God of Love, and whose Presence we experience in our awareness of the operation of the Holy Spirit in our lives. Indeed, there is no more noble, no more satisfying, no more nourishing and edifying source of spiritual strength than the pure, unadulterated praise of God!

The praise of God takes a number of forms, including:

Singing

Singing is one of the main ways of praising God. No one who has shared in singing in a large congregation of enthusiastic worshippers can doubt this! Singing is related to the Christian doctrines of creation, since we acknowledge that the use of our voices is one of God's greatest gifts to mankind. Acknowledging God as our Creator, we use our voices in order to render praise. The youth choir in that village church in the Caribbean certainly was using the divine gift of music very well as a means of praising God.

Many of the Psalms were songs of praise used in worship at the Temple in Israel. Indeed, a number of our hymns of praise are really Psalms which have been adapted for worship in a modern setting. Consider, for instance, the Scottish paraphrase of the hundredth Psalm:

All people that on earth do dwell,

Sing to the LORD with cheerful voice:

Him serve with mirth, His praise forth tell:

Come ye before Him and rejoice.

Clapping

The clapping of the hands is another way of praising God in worship. Very often, clapping accompanies singing. Clapping, which has often been associated with the more "charismatic" forms of worship, is becoming accepted in the more liturgical traditions. Significantly, clapping plays an important part in worship in ancient Israel. One of the major enthronement Psalms begins:

"Clap your hands, all ye nations . Acclaim our God with shouts of joy" (Psalm 47:1) NEB).

Lifting the hands

Very closely related to, and often accompanying clapping is the lifting of hands in praise. Again, while it has been perceived of as a method which is used in "charismatic" worship, it is gaining wide acceptance among all Christian denominations. Significantly, it too has Biblical sanction:

> *"Come, bless the LORD, all you servants of the LORD who stand by night in the house of the LORD! Lift up your hands in the holy place, and bless the LORD!""* (Psalm 134:1-1)

Playing of Musical Instruments

The praise of God in worship is greatly enhanced by the use of musical instruments. In modern Western Christianity, the organ has been the main instrument used in worship. Today, however, with the coming of "the Third Church," many more instruments are being accepted as authentic means of rendering praise to God. These include the guitar, trumpet, drums, and other percussion instruments such as the tambourine, in addition to the instrument which is traditionally used in worship - the organ! There is strong warrant in Scripture for the use of many musical instruments, which can be verified by even a cursory reading of Psalms. Psalm 150, for instance, mentions at least half a dozen musical instruments.

Dancing

Dancing is another method of worship, which is becoming more recognized in contemporary worship. Here again, there is Biblical sanction. For, it is recorded that David "danced before the Lord" (II Samuel 6:14). Significantly, in churches of many varied denominations, dancing is being utilized in worship. Indeed, churches "all over the world", in their efforts to appeal to youth, are seeking to make the worship of God an interesting and exciting experience, which will attract the younger generation.

Worship as Affirmation

In all discussions on corporate worship, it is of paramount importance always to bear in mind that it is essentially a dialogue between the worshipping community and the LORD. Together with leader(s) and congregation join in offering to God. Thus, if worship is to be truly effective, then, there must be rapport and communication between the one who leads in worship and the members of his/her congregation. Indeed, it is a corporate experience in which they draw inspiration from God and are uplifted as they worship together. Anyone who has participated in an inspiring service can testify to the validity of this fact.

This is precisely why there is provision for some form of response by the congregation in most orders of service. There are readings of Scriptures where the leader and congregation read verses alternatively. Or, there are written responses for the congregation in some liturgical traditions, which correspond to a bidding by the leader(s).

In some worship services, depending on their approach to divine worship, there is a strong element of spontaneous response. Thus, during the prayers, after the singing of a hymn or selection by the choir or soloist, or during the sermon, members of the congregation may respond audibly with shouts of "AMEN" (which is Hebrew for "So be it!") or with HALLELUJAH! (which means "PRAISE THE LORD" in Hebrew!) Sometimes, the sound is not so audible or the response may simply be by nodding in approval. When a member of the congregation responds in this way, they are participating in worship of God, and indeed, assisting the leader in offering up worship to God. It is noteworthy that in virtually all forms of worship today, the importance of affirmation is being more and more widely accepted.

Prayer

There are a number of ways whereby human beings seek to engage in their most exalted task - the praise of Almighty God. But, as has been demonstrated throughout the ages, prayer is the most effective, the most frequently used, the most profound and the most deeply satisfying way of giving expression to the human yearning to praise God. As we have seen, it is true, that praise is at the heart of worship. Moreover, as we participate in prayer day by day, and draw nearer to God, we come to realize, that praise is an essential element of prayer.

Thus, as we begin prayer, we are naturally led to offer praise to the God of our salvation. Let us, then consider some reasons why it is so important to include the element of praise in our prayer.

First, praise forms a most fitting introduction to prayer. Our prayer, if it is to be meaningful and spiritually uplifting should begin with a word of praise, of acknowledging God's Divine Creativity and that He is the one who sustains and redeems us. As we offer praise to God, we are led to worship God our Creator, to praise Christ our Redeemer and to be aware of the guidance of the Holy Spirit, our Comforter. In prayer, we praise God for Who he is.

The offering of praise, at the very beginning of worship is similar to the expression of greetings of deference at the human level. When we meet a prominent person, it is proper to acknowledge his or her position in society by addressing him/her in a particular way. We appropriately acknowledge persons who hold positions of authority in the State or Church by using special designated titles to address them - Your Highness, His/Her Excellency, "Sir", "His Holiness", etc.

If we are so deferential and careful in addressing human leaders, high in earthly positions, but subject to human frailty and weaknesses, then how much more is it necessary for us to be most courteous as we approach the One who is King of kings, LORD of lords and the only Ruler of princes!

The ancient Israelites were deeply conscious of the need for humility in approaching God. The awareness of the holiness of God caused them to enter His presence with humble, contrite hearts. Thus Moses had to take off his shoes in the Divine presence. And Isaiah, in the Temple, trembled as he heard the cry:

"Holy, holy, holy is the LORD of hosts! (Isaiah 6:3)

The ancients knew what it was to be humble in the presence of God. If we are to "walk humbly before God" as the prophet Micah exhorts (Micah 6:8), then we must approach God in an attitude of humility. We must offer to Him our allegiance and render Him the praise which is due to Him as Creator and Sustainer of the universe.

Indeed, throughout the ages, prayer has been marked by a very strong element of praise in the opening phrases. For example, as we read the prayers, of the Puritans, we are impressed by the way in which they include the offering of praise to God. The element of praise is also very strong in the prayers of such religious leaders as St. Francis of Assisi, St. Theresa, Martin Luther, and John Wesley.

Yes, our forefathers in the faith knew what it was to be humble in the presence of God. Thus a strong element of praise characterized their prayers. It is not always so prominent in the prayers we offer today. Yet, if our prayer life is to be truly meaningful and effective, we must recapture something of this element of humility before God in our prayer. If we are able to attain this objective and enrich our prayer life, then we must "walk humbly with thy God" as Micah exhorts (Micah 6:8). We must approach our God in an attitude of humility and offer our allegiance, rendering to the Divine One the praise which is due Him as Creator and Sustainer of the Universe. We must take seriously the challenge of the Psalm:

"O magnify the LORD with me, and let us exalt his name together" (Psalms 34:3)

Moreover, because we love the company of our fellowmen, it is very important to note that the element of praise figures prominently in corporate worship. Indeed, when prayer is offered by or on behalf of a congregation, it is the element of praise which, most often, predominates.

This is precisely because when we get together we are inspired to offer praise to God and to acknowledge His greatness.

Let us reflect for a moment on one of the great Psalms of praise, Psalm 95. It is known as the "Venite," which means "Come." This deeply inspiring song of praise which has been used in worship for many centuries both in Israel and in the Church, begins with the invitation to worship:

"O come, Let us sing unto the LORD; let us make a joyful noise to the rock of our salvation. Let us come before His presence with thanksgiving, and make a joyful noise unto Him with psalms" (vs 2).

This invitation to praise is such that the worshiper can hardly resist it. The person who enters into the spirit of this Psalm cannot help but praise God. The Psalm draws us into the Presence of God, and we are thus led to praise the LORD, quite naturally.

The Psalm continues with an acknowledgment of the greatness of God:

"For the LORD is a great God and a great King above all gods. In his hand are all the deep places of the earth: the strength of the hills is his also" (vs 3).

Note the strong rejection of idolatry here. He alone is the God who is worthy to be praised. The ancient Hebrews feared the sea. Thus the greatness of God the Creator is manifested in the fact that the sea is His and He made it and His hands formed the dry land.

With all this in mind, the Psalm climaxes in the exhortation:

"O come, let us worship and bow down: let us kneel before the LORD our Maker" (vs 6).

Here the praise of God naturally leads to prayer. As the worshipper accepts the invitation to worship the LORD, and acknowledges the greatness of God, there is no response he/she can make but to fall on their knees and enter into the praise of God. Yes, the praise of God leads us ultimately to fall upon our knees in prayer to our Maker. Truly, prayer is praise!

One very good thing about praise is the fact that it does lift us out of ourselves, out of our concerns for our own failings and weaknesses and points us upward to God, the Source of our Strength. Thus, the praise of God, offered in the context of fervent prayer is a very powerful antidote to depression and self- pity. So often, when we feel lonely, when we have been hurt by someone else, when we have failed in some great undertaking, or when ill, we become subject to self- pity and depression. In such moments, it is essential that we should offer praise to God! And in so doing, we are lifted from the depths of depressed feelings to the heights of joy and ecstasy in the presence of the LORD.

In Psalm 130, for instance, we have a clear illustration of this elevating power of praise. The Psalmist, in a depressed frame of mind, cries:

> *"Out of the depths have I cried unto thee, O LORD! Lord, hear my voice: let thine ears be attentive to the voice of my supplications!"* *(Psalms 130:8)*

The cause of his downcast state of mind we do not know. No doubt, in some way he had offended God and was deeply conscious of his sinful act, which had driven a wedge between himself and his Maker. Nevertheless, he remembers that God is merciful. Continuing, he reflects upon the forgiveness of God and places himself entirely at the disposal of his merciful God. Evidently, his prayer is answered. Thus, in the closing verses he is able to proclaim:

> *"Let Israel, hope in the LORD! For with the LORD there is mercy, and with Him is plenteous redemption"* *(Psalms 1130::8).*

The Psalmist, who begins this prayer in the depths of despair is willing to complete it by exhorting others with a word of hope, and praising God for His wonderful redemptive works. It is the praise of God which helps him to be lifted "out of the depths."

In several other Psalms we see a similar dynamic at work. A person goes to God in prayer with a dejected and deeply burdened spirit. In this state, he or she begins to reflect upon the ways in which God has demonstrated His redemptive action in human experience. This reflection of God's saving activity leads the person to praise the LORD. Psalm 22, for instance, which begins with the famous Cry of Dereliction, ends with the Psalmist proclaiming his willingness to praise the LORD in the congregation of the righteous. Likewise in Psalm 57, a cry of anguish ends up as a prayer of praise.

So often it is the case that the person who begins to offer prayer, burdened and weighed down by the pains, problems and trials of this transitory life, is lifted literally "out of the depths" and is released from the bondage of these tribulations simply by the offer of praise to God. In earnest prayer, clear answers to complex problems are revealed, long kept and "bottled up" anxieties are relieved, the guilt inflicting burden of sin is lifted, the sublime joy of "forgiveness and reconciliation" is experienced, and, the sicknesses which afflict the body, mind and soul, are healed. In this sense, prayer may be truly described as "therapeutic." It is precisely for this reason that the profound writer of the Epistle of James exhorts us:

> *"Is there anyone who is ill? He should send for the church elders, who will pray for him and rub olive oil on him in the name of the LORD. This prayer made in faith will heal the sick person; the LORD will restore him to health, and the sins he has committed will be forgiven. So, then, confess your sins to one another and pray for one another, so that you will be healed. The prayer of a good person has a powerful effect"* (James 5:14-16 NEB).

Dear reader, perhaps you are "down in the dumps." Perhaps, even as you read these lines, you are facing some serious problems in your own life, which threaten your physical, mental and spiritual well being - crippling debts, a broken marriage, children who are estranged from you, problems on your job, the acute pain of the loss of a loved one, or the ravages of a debilitating disease. If so, then NOW is the time to praise the LORD. Even though the circumstances of life may be difficult for you, you are exhorted, not to seek to escape from them in prayer, but to place these mundane concerns before the LORD as you draw near to Him.

Yes, in this "sweet hour of prayer", as you enter into the inner chamber of deep communion with God, you will be lifted up "out

of the depths" of despair and pain into the heights of sublime joy
and peace which is the unique experience of those who dwell
continually "in the Presence of the LORD."

> *"Thou dost show me the path of life; in thy presence there is*
> *fullness of joy, in thy right hand are pleasures for evermore"*
> (Psalm 16:11).

Let us, then, as we come to the end of this chapter remember
to render praise to God continually, in prayer, that we may be
lifted: From anxiety to peacefulness, From despair to hope, From
sickness to health, From fear to faith; Yea, from the "wages of sin",
which is death to the gift of God-in-Christ, which is eternal life,
Amen.

3

*P*RAYER
*I*S
*T*HANKSGIVING

There is another important thing about the praise of God, It is this: *Praise naturally leads to thanks-giving.* It is very easy to understand why this is so.

As we have seen, when we praise God we are led to think of the ways in which he has helped and strengthened us over the years. Every way in which he has been good to us. Indeed, it is not too much to suggest that praise and thanksgiving are inextricably bound up with the other. This is why we so often tend to confuse them and to speak as if praise and thanksgiving are the same. They are related, but they are to be distinguished from each other if we are to grow in our devotional life. Let us, then, reflect on the relationship between these two vitally important elements of prayer.

When we praise God we acknowledge His greatness, His majesty, His holiness and His power. Like Isaiah in the Temple, we are overcome by the concept of His Holiness, that quality which is so distinctive of the Godhead. The sense of the holiness of God overwhelms us in such moments of adoration that we can do nothing but burst forth in praise of the Almighty God of Creation. (See Isaiah 6). This outpouring of praise in response to the contemplation of Divine Sovereignty is well brought out in a great hymns of praise:

"Praise to the LORD, the Almighty, the King of Creation; O my soul, praise Him, for He is thy health and salvation; All ye who hear, brothers and sisters, draw near, Praise Him in glad adoration."

When we consider what God has done for us, in us and through us, then we are led to thank Him. Or, to put it another way, praise comes first and it is followed by thanksgiving. We praise God before we thank Him. But we thank Him because we can praise Him! Concisely, thanksgiving is a logical consequence to praise.

This close relationship between praise and thanksgiving is constantly brought out in the great hymns of praise of the Bible - the Psalms. Let us examine, for instance, Psalm 100 in a modern translation.

This Psalm, as has been pointed out, has been paraphrased and used as a hymn of Praise in Christian worship, is essentially an invocation, a call to the congregation gathered to participate enthusiastically in the worship of God. Thus, it begins: "Sing to the LORD, all the world! Worship the LORD with joy; Come before Him with happy songs." (GNB)

The basis for praise is to be found in the next verse:

"Know ye that the LORD, he is God; it is he that hath made us, and not we ourselves, we are his people and the sheep of his hand" (vs3).

Note how the elements of praise and thanksgiving are so skillfully woven together in the consecutive verse:

"Enter into his gates with thanksgiving, and into his courts with praise, be thankful unto him and bless his name" (vs 4).

This invocation is nothing other than an invitation to the congregation to enter fully into the spirit of worship by offering praise and thanks to God. Indeed, who can read these verses in a sensitive manner, without bursting forth into praise and the offering of thanks to God, the Holy One, the Bountiful Provider?

There is no wonder that it concludes with the proclamation: "The LORD is good; His love is eternal and His faithfulness lasts for ever."

It is abundantly clear that there is a very close link between praise and thanksgiving. Both are essential to meaningful, Christian worship, of which prayer is such an important aspect. We have concentrated on praise in the previous chapter, let us now think more about thanksgiving.

In thanksgiving, we list the ways in which God has been good to us and thank Him for His benefits to us. Very significantly, in Biblical teaching and the history of the Church, there is the constant reminder to us to give thanks to God, and not to be ungrateful for the many benefits and blessings of which we have been the recipients. (Exodus 15; Deut. 6:4-9; Deut. 12:1-12; Psalm 9; 136; Col. 3:12-17; Rev. 7: 12).

The importance of thanksgiving, of being appreciative of what God has done for us, is brought vividly to us in one of the miracles of healing of Jesus. Recorded for us in the Gospel of St. Luke, this episode begins with ten lepers imploring Jesus to heal them. The Master sends them to the priests, and on their way they are cleansed from their dreaded disease. Amazingly, only one of them returns to give thanks to Jesus for having received such a great miracle of healing. He is a Samaritan. The response of Jesus is at once intriguing and instructive:

> *"Jesus said, There were ten men who were healed; where are the other nine? Why is this foreigner the only one who came back to give thanks to God?"* (Luke 17:17-18 NEB)

There can be no doubt that thanksgiving should form an extremely important part of our prayer life. Indeed, whether we pray for long hours every day or short periods. Whether we find the mornings or evenings more convenient for prayer, and whatever may be our religious background, it is incumbent upon us to bear in mind CONTINUALLY the reasons why we should offer thanks to God.

Here is just a short list of reasons for thanking God:

- Life and health.

- The property which is entrusted to us. Some success we have recently experienced.

- Our family and friends.

- The provision of food for our bodies.

- Freedom to worship as we would like.

- The fellowship we enjoy as members of the Church, the body of Christ.

- For employment. Salvation which is ours in Jesus Christ.

- The order, beauty and constancy of nature

This list is very short indeed, and, no doubt, you would have no difficulty in doubling it!

No matter how bad our situation might appear to be, no matter how many pains and frustrations we may bear, no matter how "unfortunate" our circumstances may be, still we can find something to thank God for. This is important for us to remember because we can become complacent and take much for granted. Or we may sink into self-pity and think that our lot in life is worst than that of anyone else we know. Here we can be greatly helped in our Christian endeavor by reflecting on the experiences we have day by day.

I recall a prominent layman telling me many years ago, that at the end of each day he would tabulate the negative and positive experiences he had. First, he would think of the negative and bad experiences and he would regard them as the "minus experiences." Then, he would reflect upon the good things which had taken place and he would call them "the plus experiences."

Then he testified with a twinkle in his eyes, "and you know, Reverend, the pluses always add up to more than the minuses! Always!"

My brother, my sister, is this not true of your life? Have you not found that despite all the negative and difficult experiences you have had to face, the LORD still has somehow brought you through them? Indeed, have you not discovered that there is much "food for thought" and profound truth in that old saying:

"Count your blessings, name them one by one, And it will surprise you what the LORD has done!"

Years ago, while a student at theological college in Jamaica, I used to stay with a Minister and his family during my holidays. The Minister's little daughter was sometimes called upon to say grace. Inevitably, she would repeat this well known grace as we sat for our meal: "

God is great

God is good

Let us thank Him for our food. Amen."

This little child's grace (as is so often the case with devotions designed for children) has a message which we all need to take to heart. For, it helps us to appreciate both the close tie and the clear distinction between praise and thanksgiving. God is great, there-fore, we must praise Him. God is good, therefore, we must thank Him. Yes, praise God because of whom He is - Holy, Creator, Sustainer. We thank God for what he has done and continues to do for us, in us and through us. Indeed, praise and thanksgiving are different sides of the same coin - worship.

In the course of this transitory life, there will be trials and tribulations. We will have to face difficult situations, since it is so true that "life is not a bed of roses." There will be times when we shall face problems in our homes and family life, in our marriages, in our finances, and even in our spiritual endeavor. There will be trials and temptations which will test our faith. In such moments, it is important for us to remember the benefits we have received and "to count our blessings."

The ancient Israelites, in their moments of despair, when pressed by the foe, were inspired as they recalled their experiences of God's salvation as demonstrated in the Exodus and the great battles of deliverance as recorded in their history, the Heilsgeschichte, salvation history. Likewise, we should recall the ways in which God has blessed us in the past and as we render thanks for them we shall find strength to continue our earthly endeavors. So shall we be enabled to offer praise and thanks to God even in the midst of adversity.

Through all the changing scenes of life,

In trouble and in joy,

The praises of my God shall still

My heart and tongue employ.

What then, can we say about the element of thanksgiving? Surely, it is the realization that thanksgiving should form an integral part of our prayer. Our prayer should be filled with thanksgiving no matter what our situation in life may be. The offering of thanks will greatly enrich our prayer life. More profoundly, our whole life in all aspects should be characterized by an attitude of thankfulness.

There was a Christian gentleman, who, when asked, 'How are you?' would respond, inevitably, with the most thought provoking answer, "MUCH TO BE THANKFUL FOR!" This was his answer whether he was feeling "on top of the world" or on his sick bed! What a superb example of the thankful attitude which should inform the life of every Christian!

Beloved, since, as we have seen, there is always "something to thank God for," then our lives should be characterized by an attitude which is always thankful and filled with a sense of gratitude to our Covenant God. Our Loving God, "who for us men and our salvation was made Man." So, then, whatever our circumstances may be, no matter how bitter or painful may be our experiences, in the midst of most extreme trials and tribulations, we should still demonstrate that attitude which is marked by thankfulness to God. St. Paul, as usual, has some very sound advice for us:

> *"Let Christ's peace be arbiter in your hearts. And be filled with gratitude. Let the message of Christ dwell among you in all its richness. Instruct and admonish one another with the utmost wisdom. Sing thankfully in your hearts to God with Psalms and hymns and spiritual songs. Whatever you are doing, whether you speak or act, do everything in the name of the LORD Jesus, giving thanks to God and the Father through Him." (Col. 3:16-17).*

Yes, prayer is thanksgiving.

SOME SUGGESTED QUESTIONS AND EXERCISES

1. What is prayer? How would you answer this question?

2. Look at the list of definitions of prayer on page one, which two would you select as being the most suitable definitions of prayer?

3. Do you agree that prayer is the soul's sincere desire uttered or unexpressed?

4. Write a short prayer which includes the elements of praise and thanksgiving.

5. What is the difference between praise and thanksgiving in prayer?

6. In what ways would you like to see the prayer life of your Church improve?

7. Consider prayerfully the possibility of starting a prayer group in your home.

8. Why is it stated that: "Confession is good for the soul?"

4

*P*RAYER *I*S *P*ETITION

"Thou art coming to a King, great petitions with thee bring."
"Therefore, I tell you, whatever you ask in prayer, believe that you
have received it, and it will be yours." The power of prayer is great
indeed! - Mark 11: 24 RSV Throughout the ages, people "from all
walks of life" - saints and sinners, rich and poor, black and white,
old and young - have all experienced the great spiritual power
which comes through and in prayer.

Prayer unlocks the gates of heaven. In prayer we draw near to
God with a humble contrite heart. Yes, in prayer we draw near to
God and ask Him those things which we most earnestly desire.
The Bible gives many illustrations of those who came to God with
their request and received that for which they had prayed.

Take, for instance, Hannah. One of the two wives of Elkanah,
a devout Hebrew, she was a woman who suffered for many years
from the social disgrace (at that time!) of not having any children.
(For the woman of those times who had no children was despised
and subjected to several social pressures). Her anguish at not
being able to bear any children was compounded by the fact that
her rival ("other wife") sarcastically jeered her because of her
barren state. Indeed, it is hard for today's "liberated woman" to
understand the extent of her pain and the sense of anguish,
frustration and even rejection!

It was in this depressed state that Hannah entered the Temple
and prayed to God for the gift of a son. The Scriptures record the
incident with these moving words:

"*One day, after they had finished their meal in the home of the LORD at Shiloh, Hannah got up. She was deeply distressed and she cried bitterly as she prayed to the LORD:*

'Almighty God! Look at me, your servant! See my trouble and remember me! Don't forget me! If you give me a son, I promise that I will dedicate him to you for his whole life......."

"*As she prayed, so bitterly distressed, with lips moving and no audible words, the old priest, Eli, observing, guessed that she might have been drinking too much. Sternly he admonished her::*

Stop making a drunken show of yourself! Stop your drinking and sober up!

No Sir. I'm not drunk Sir" *she answered.*

'I haven't been drinking. I'm desperate and I have been praying pouring out my troubles to the LORD (I Samuel 1:14-15, GNB).

What an apt and moving description of the prayer of petition! In prayer, we draw to God in the most intimate way and reveal him to the depths of our hearts, our highest heights, our deepest hurts, our most intimate secrets, our deepest sorrows and our greatest joys. Petition is pouring out our heart to the LORD.

The priest understood her situation. He bid her leave the temple and expressed his own desire that her prayer should be answered:

"*Go and may the LORD grant you your petition*" (I Samuel 1:17 GNB).

And so it was, that in the fullness of time, her prayer was answered. She had a son. In accord with her vow, she dedicated him to the LORD. That child grew to become one of the greatest religious leaders of all time - Samuel. No wonder! He was conceived as a result of prayer, nurtured in an atmosphere of prayer and himself was a man of prayer!

Hannah was a woman of faith! She believed that God could and would answer prayer. It was in this confidence that she approached Him, and, in persistence, she received, that which she requested.

The earnest pleading of Hannah to God for a son, a plea born out of deep anguish in very trying circumstances, highlights dramatically and most clearly, the essential nature of one of the most important elements of prayer - petition. This word, which is derived from the Latin word for "request," expresses something which is to be found in most of our prayers - the making of requests to God.

In Medieval times, when the Monarchy had much more executive authority than at present, it was often used by the subject in making requests of their king or queen. Something of this element still survives in our understanding of the word, which is defined as "Formal request to a superior or one in authority for some favor, privilege, redress of a grievance, or the like!" In the Judicial system, this aspect is clear when, an attorney "prays" for mercy on behalf of a client.

This aspect of prayer is so strong that it often prevails over all the others. Thus, if you were to ask some people "What is prayer?" especially those who do not have much of a religious background, their answer might be, "That's asking God for things!" And while those who are of a sensitive nature might not be happy about such a pragmatic way of looking at prayer, humanly speaking, such an answer can hardly be too strongly contested. For, in prayer, we do make known our needs to God. In this sense, it is not too much to state that "prayer is petition." If this is so, what can we say about this element of prayer?

First, it has to be said that petition is the most natural and spontaneous aspect of prayer. When people find themselves in a most desperate situation - in a storm, shipwreck, in an accident, or deeply in debt - even those who claim "not to be religious" as a last resort, may turn to God in prayer. We all know or have heard stories of pilots, having engine trouble, land their plane "on a wing and a prayer!"

This universal element of prayer as petition, asking the Deity for help in most desperate situations, is evident in the Biblical incident recorded in the Book of Jonah. Jonah was seeking to flee from the presence of God. Commanded to go to Nineveh in the east, he took a ship heading for Tarshish, in the west! While he was "on board", there was a terrible storm which caused the boat to be cast to and fro upon the waves. In this situation, the pagan sailors all prayed for safety to their gods. They also urged Jonah, scolding him, "Arise, call upon thy God!" (Jonah 1:6)

Yes, even the most irreligious of persons, when things get tough, will turn to God in prayer. Petition, For the Christian, however, is based upon the conviction that God is good. In this respect, it is very closely related to thanksgiving. As we have noted, when we give God thanks, we do so on the basis of the conviction that He is good and caring. By the same token, when we come to God and make our request known to Him in the context of petitions, we do so on the basis of the conviction that he is good and that he really cares for us.

Here the Master, who Himself, was constantly in prayer to God, has a very instructive word for us. In several passages, he reminds us of the goodness of God the heavenly Father, who cares for us. Thus, in the Sermon on the Mount, he declares that the God who cares for the sparrows and the lilies of the field, has a very special concern for mankind. (Matt. 6:28-34). Again, in the treatise on prayer in Luke's Gospel, He notes that an earthly father has the wisdom and care to provide for the needs of his children. (Luke 11:10-13). Since God is a good God, then we can confidently approach Him and place before Him our needs and our deepest concerns, our greatest anxieties and our deepest pains.

Trust in God is the very basis of petition. We approach God trusting Him. We believe that He is good and will hear us. Thus, in prayer we should be bold. This is extremely important for us to bear in mind! We must be bold and quite specific. Here the case of Hannah is most instructive. When Hannah prayed to God, she made it abundantly clear what she wanted - a son. She had been harassed by her rival, who day by day ridiculed her because she had no child. She was ostracized by other women because she was barren. Indeed, there must have been those who implied, like the friends of Job that she was in some way to blame for her condition. She was cursed with barrenness! So, when she approached God, she did so boldly. She came and requested a son. She was bold and she was specific.

In our prayers of petition we should be bold and specific It is not enough for us to be vague in our prayer, especially in making known our requests to God!

Because prayer is petition, pleading with God, seeking His intervention into our lives, His guidance in making our decisions, then there is no limit to the concerns which we may bring before God as we come to him in an attitude of prayer. The list below, which is by no means exhaustive, includes just some of these concerns including:

1.   Prayers for health and healing - Under this broad heading we would include the many prayers which are offered for the illnesses which bring suffering to mankind. In the contemporary situation, we think especially of those suffering from AIDS.

2.   Prayers for prosperity and financial security - There are the concerns of people with regard to their financial condition with special prayers for deliverance from debt.

3.   Happiness.

4.   Success in examinations.

5.   Fertility - Prayers by married couples who are childless and anxious for children. We may call these "Hannah prayers."

6.   Prayer for a home

7.   Prayer for a suitable life partner.

8.   Prayer for employment.

9.   Closely related to the prayer for employment is for promotion on one's job.

10.   Prayer to loose weight.

11.   Prayer for safety on a journey - by land, sea, or air.

12.   Prayer for self-control.

13.   Prayer for moral guidance.

14.   Prayer for spiritual growth - Deeper spirituality to overcome temptations and the wandering mind in prayer.

Moreover, the Bible consistently and clearly teaches that our prayer life should be marked by persistence and steadfastness. It is not enough to just pray once or twice and then dismiss prayer as "ineffective" when one's request is not granted. Rather, it is essential that our prayer should be carried out constantly and diligently. Concisely, we should not give up easily in prayer.

Consider Hannah! She did not go to the temple at Shiloh and pray once. Rather, as she went to that holy place year by year, she poured out her heart in earnest prayer to God for a son. Indeed, if we examine the text carefully, we cannot but come to the conclusion that she was a woman of prayer, who spent hours day by day on her knees. Likewise, the great religious leaders of Israel were given much to prayer. Thus Abraham, Moses and the prophets were constantly on the prayer line. One thinks, of Elijah, who by means of prayer wrought great victories for the LORD (1st Kings 17:19-22; 18: 20-46).

As we examine the New Testament pictures of the Master, we find him constantly in prayer and it is noted that it was His daily custom to begin the day in communion with His heavenly Father. (Mark 1:35-37).

And, most significantly, in His Parables, he constantly exhorted His disciples to practice persistence in prayer. Thus, in that dramatic Parable of the Friend at Midnight, (Luke 11:5-8) He tells of a man who had a late night visitor with nothing to offer him! Desperately and to avoid embarrassment, he goes to the home of a friend and keeps on banging at the door until the friend arises and gives him what he requires! The Master, perceptively observes that it was not because of friendship that the man arose and gave him the loaf he needed; it was because of his persistence or his "importunity" as the King James Version puts it. The New English

Bible brings out the lesson very well for us in language which is more relevant to us:

"I tell you that even if he will not provide for him out of friendship, the very shamelessness of the request will make him get up and give him all he needs (Luke 11:8 NEB)

The man was so utterly disgusted with the constant banging on his door, that he just got up and gave his friend the loaf that he wanted for entertaining the one who coming to be his house guest late that night! In this dramatic way Jesus drives home the importance of persistence in prayer. He also makes the same point in an equally graphic parable, in which a harsh judge is worn down by a persistent widow and thus forced to give in to her request (Luke 18:1-8).

These virtues, boldness and persistence in prayer, are solidly based on a principle which is absolutely essential for effectiveness in petition - sincerity. This word implies purity, lack of guile or anything which is deceptive. There is an important point for us all here! In our ordinary everyday living, and in our relationships with others, we often tend to be reluctant to reveal our true needs. We may find ourselves in a situation in where we may be "dying from hunger," but when offered a meal may refuse it with a polite "No thank you." Or we may want to impress others with our wealth by spending much, while we are, deeply in debt. We may even adopt "double standards," appearing to live an upright life in one situation, but being quite the opposite. No wonder Shakespeare so aptly observed:

"All the world's a stage and all the men and women merely players!"

He was right! For so often in life we put on a "big show" in order to impress our fellowmen. But, when we come to God none of this pretence is necessary! We can afford to come to Him and let Him know our deepest needs. We can approach Him and make our requests known to Him, confident that He will hear us. This is precisely why we need to be bold and persistent in making our requests known to God. If we are in need of a job, then, in prayer let us ask Him to provide for us. Indeed, there are many ways in which we may be in need of divine assistance. We may be facing problems in our marriage, may be too fat, may be deeply in debt....whatever our condition, in petition we can let God know and we can also speak to Him confident that he will hear us! Yes, it is true! Thou art coming to a King, Great petitions with thee bring.

Let us, as we come to the end of this chapter, return to the scene with which we began - Hannah earnestly praying for a son. In her prayer, she demonstrated all the qualities which make for effectiveness in the prayer of petition - faith, boldness, persistence, and most of all sincerity. She believed that God, the God of her fathers, could and would answer prayer. It was in this confidence that she approached God and as a result she received what she asked for.

And what of you, my dear friend? As you go about, are there great unfulfilled desires in your life? Do you have needs which seem to become greater and greater as the days go by? Are you frustrated and about "to give up on prayer" because your prayers have not been answered? Then, I must urge you, "Don't give up!" This is the time that you must "Hold on." Pray in confidence that the Great and Good God who is the Creator, the God of Abraham, Isaac and Jacob, will answer you and grant your petitions. Yes, like Hannah, you must be willing to pray without ceasing.

"O what joy we often forfeit. O what needless pain we bear. All because we do not carry Everything to God in prayer."

A MOTHER WHO PRAYED

A young mother smiled proudly as she confidently heldher first-born in her arms for the first time! She had every reason to be proud and happy. For he was a fine, bouncing baby boy!

As she held the new born baby and while her husband also proudly beamed with joy, she offered a special prayer, quietly to God. It was a prayer of petition. Like Hannah she prayed that her son would grow up to become a full time servant of the LORD. And, like Mary, she kept this petition a secret for a long time.

Eventually, when the child grew up, the time came when he was conscious of a Call from God to serve in the ministry of His Church. He responded and became a Minister of the Gospel. It was not until after he had served for some years in the ministry that his mother revealed to him the content of her prayer at his birth.

In giving his testimony, this Minister continues to encourage mothers to pray for their children at birth, to offer prayer that their children might serve the LORD in one of the many ministries of the Church.

Today, the leaders of many church bodies complain that there are not enough young people coming forward to offer to serve as priests, ministers and deacons. Indeed, the situation is serious in some churches with the average age of the clergy being well over fifty. There is an urgent need for young people "to fill the gaps."

Are you a young mother or father who has just experienced the joy of having "a little addition" to your family? Then, do not fail to offer prayer constantly for your child. Yes, pray that he/she may grow up to be a true and faithful soldier of Christ, the Master. There can be no doubt that many more young people would offer themselves for the ministry of the Church if more parents were to offer prayers at birth dedicating their children to the service of the LORD!

5

*P*RAYER

*I*S

*C*ONFESSION

"If we say that we have no sin, we deceive ourselves and the truth is not in us, but if we confess our sins, he is faithful and just to forgive us our sins, and to cleanse us from all unrighteousness" (1 John 1:8-9).

"CONFESSION IS GOOD FOR THE SOUL!" There can be no doubt that this old adage contains a great truth. For confession, the acknowledging of sinfulness, is indeed essential for our spiritual well being.

Since prayer is vital for spiritual growth, it can be asserted, without reservation, that confession is a fundamental aspect of prayer. In previous chapters, we have seen that prayer includes the elements of praise, thanksgiving and petition. Prayer is also confession! In this chapter, let us ponder the reason why confession is so necessary, examine its meaning and seek to discover ways in which we can improve the effectiveness of our own prayer life, and our relationships with God and man.

Here it is important to realize that first of all, confession has to do with our relationship to God. As human beings we live day by day in relationship with others - our family, our friends, our employers, our fellowmen and the people that we meet in various situations. Our relationships to these people are very important to us as social beings. Our lives are deeply affected by these encounters with others. However, from the Christian perspective, the supreme relationship, that which governs all others, is our relationship with God. Thus, the most important question that a person can ask himself or herself is, "How can I get right with God?"

It is precisely when we ask this question that we realize and are deeply conscious of the fact that we are not in right relationship with our Maker, that a gulf exists between God and ourselves.

What is the reason for this awareness of a broken relationship with God? The answer - SIN. Sin, the violation of the Divine law, causes a break in our relationship with God. As the late Professor Paul Tillich so often reminded us, it is sin which is the cause of estrangement between God and man.

There are deliberate sins that we commit when we knowingly transgress law of God - when we steal, commit adultery, lie or murder. Then there are the sins which we commit unwittingly. These are sometimes known as "sins of omission." Whether they are done deliberately or inadvertently, they are still acts of violation of the law of God and as Carl Menninger has demonstrated, such acts do lead to a breaking of our relationship with God.

When our relationship with God is marred in this way, what can we do? Well, if the relationship is to be restored, then the first thing that we must do is to ADMIT our guilt, to take responsibility for what we have done. To put it bluntly, confession is essential because, in the words of the prophet Isaiah, "We all have sinned and come short of the glory of God."

There can be no doubt that it is never ever easy for anyone to admit guilt. A school boy once made a promise to help the members of his class with a project on a Saturday morning. However, when the day came he simply decided not to do so;

instead he stayed at home. On the Monday that followed his teacher rebuked him for not turning up to help as he had promised. The little boy felt very sorry and was made to apologize for it.

Because it is not easy to admit that we have done wrong, there is a tendency, all-too-human and too frequently engaged in, for us to try our best "to cover up" our sins and to make excuses. So often we want to plead, like the man in Court, "guilty with explanation." And so we try to excuse ourselves for what we had done by laying the blame upon others or other institutions. So we blame our background, society, the Government, the Church, our friends....anyone but ourselves. There is small wonder that we act in this way. In so doing we are truly "the children of Adam."

In the Biblical incident of the Fall, Adam and Eve sinned by disobedience. When God rebuked Adam for disobedience, he shirked the responsibility of admitting guilt by stating that he had been led into temptation by the woman God gave to him, who in turn, blamed it all on the serpent! (Gen. 3:9-14). Talk about "passing the buck!"

No, it is not enough for us to seek to blame others for our sins and mistakes. In most cases, when we try to do so, we really should be looking at ourselves. True, there are occasions in which we are not to be held responsible for our actions, when "circumstances beyond our control" are involved. But, in most cases we are individually responsible for our sins.

In the days of the prophet Ezekiel, there were those who blamed their ancestors for their situation. They excused themselves by repeating the proverb:

> *"The fathers have eaten sour grapes, and children's teeth are set on edge"* (Ezekiel 18:2).

The prophet, however, would not allow them to continue to blame their sins on their ancestors! Rather he taught the doctrine of individual responsibility. They should not blame their ancestors for their situation; they should be responsible and prepared to acknowledge that it was their own sinful actions which led them to their predicament (Ezekiel 18:3-18).

There is much for us to learn from these Biblical incidents. Whenever we do something which is wrong, when we hurt someone's feelings, when we sin, then it is best that we acknowledge our sins before God. This is the only way in which we will be able to "get back" into a right relationship with Him. Yes, the admission of one's guilt is the first and most fundamental step in the process of confession. The purpose of confession, then, is to obtain the forgiveness of God, that we may be reconciled to Him. But confession has a deeper purpose! It is also for renewing us for further ministry and service to our fellowmen.

Thus, when we come to discuss the significance of confession in prayer, there can be no doubt that the Biblical incident of David and Bethsheba is most instructive. Indeed, it is not too much to suggest that it is found in virtually every discussion of the subject of confession. David's great prayer of Confession, as recorded in Psalm 51, has always been regarded as the model for a prayer of confession. Let us, pause, however for a moment to examine the circumstances leading up to this great prayer of Confession.

The story is told with great vividness, in the eleventh and twelfth chapters of II Samuel. The setting was the of the later years of the reign of King David. He had won great victories and had established Jerusalem as the capital of ancient Israel. David no longer went out to war; instead He sent his generals to do the fighting. There is the root of his sin! He was idle. As we so often say

"The devil finds work for idle hands."

Sitting comfortably on the roof of his palace, he saw a beautiful lady taking a bath in the afternoon and he was attracted. Enquiring, he found out that she was Bathsheba, the wife of Uriah the Hittite. He invited her to the palace and as a result of their encounter she became pregnant! Learning of this, he arranged for her husband to be placed in such a dangerous position on the battle field where he was killed!

The story is told with great sensitivity and with great attention to theological truth. Thus the duplicity and wickedness of the king stand in stark contrast to the sincerity and simple honesty of Uriah, who in utter loyalty to the king, refused to even go to his own home! So the poor man was killed. And David took the woman to be his wife!

But that was not the end of the story. By no means! As the Bible puts it, "The thing which David did displeased the LORD" (II Samuel 11:27). The king had committed the double sin of adultery and murder. Both sins were clear violations of the ancient Covenant law of Israel. The LORD, the righteous and Holy One, could not allow such blatant violation of the Divine Law to go unchecked, even if it was the king who had done so!

So the prophet Nathan, called of God, sternly rebuked the king for his action. In a vivid parable, he portrayed a rich man who had viciously robbed a poor man of his meager possession. The king, as the one responsible to execute the justice of the LORD in Israel, roundly condemned the man. Then the prophet dramatically turned upon him and charged, "Thou art the man!"

What did the king do when confronted in this way with his action? Did he seek to exercise his power by snubbing the advice of the prophet? Did he try to make excuses for his actions? Did he claim that "as king he could do as he liked?" No! He wisely did not resort to any of these.

Rather, in an act of supreme contrition, he made confession to God. In Psalm 51, which has long been attributed to David, he makes confession to God for what he has done. It may be described as the prayer of Confession "par excellence," and as such, it would be useful for us to examine it.

The major part of the Psalm may be dealt with under the following headings:

Verses 1 - 2	Cry for mercy
Verses 3 - 6	Admission of guilt
Verses 7 - 9	Prayer for cleansing (reconciliation)
Verses 10 - 17	Prayer for restoration

Verses 1-2   Cry for Mercy

This great Prayer of Confession begins appropriately with a cry for mercy. David appeals to God on the basis of His covenant love, which had been demonstrated in so many ways in his own relationship to God. He begins:

"Have mercy upon me O God, according to thy loving kindness: according unto the multitude of thy tender mercies blot out my transgressions " (vs 1).

The mercy and loving kindness of God was known to David. He appealed to God on these grounds. Let us bear in mind that the loving kindness of God was supremely manifested in the sending of His Divine Son to be our Saviour. Thus we have all the more reason to appeal to the mercy of God.

Verse 3 - 6   Act of Confession

The penitent David, having cried out to the LORD of Mercy, rapidly moves to the essential matter of his prayer - the confession of his sin. In the presence of God, like Isaiah in the Temple, he is deeply aware of his sinful condition. (Isaiah 6:4) In this most contrite frame of mind, he humbly confesses with sorrow:

"For I acknowledge my sin; and my sin is ever before me" (3).

I acknowledge my sin!" How utterly important is it for us to acknowledge that we have done wrong when we sin. The Psalmist, unlike Adam and Eve, does not attempt to shift the blame to anyone else or to make excuses for his wicked deed. He freely admits that he has done wrong. Here, we have the very heart of confession - the admission of guilt, the willingness of an individual or corporate body to take responsibility for violating the Divine Law. This is the first step to restoration of one's relationship to God after it has been breached by the commitment of sin.

The Psalmist, in his highly penitential mood, continues:

"Against thee, thee only have I sinned and done this evil in thy sight" (vs 4).

It is very important that we should take note of the Psalmist's confession here; for it has a point of profound theological significance - sin is first and foremost against God. Now, it is true that the act of David was committed against Uriah, the husband of Bathsheba. But as one reads the Biblical text, it is made abundantly clear that David and his household suffered precisely because his sin was regarded as being against God. By murdering this man and by committing adultery, the king had violated two of the most fundamental precepts of the Covenant. Yes, the king, who was expected to be the champion of Yahweh's justice, had himself committed an act of grave injustice! Thus, it is recorded, acidly, "But the thing that David had done displeased the LORD" (2 Sam. 11::27).

And, as several scholars have demonstrated it was a result of this act of violation of the Divine Law that a series of terrible judgements were visited upon the house of David. The child, which was conceived as a result of the king's adulterous act, died just a few days after birth. The royal family was plagued with instability and an act of incest. The king's favorite son led a rebellion which almost succeeded in dethroning him. These events, known as "The Succession narrative", all came as a result of David's sin.

There is one clear lesson which is expounded throughout this Narrative - God does not tolerate sin! Throughout the Bible this principle is repeated again and again. No one can read the Bible, in a sensitive manner, without being made constantly aware of the fact that it is impossible "to get away" with sin. As Numbers warns, "Be sure, your sin will find you out!" (Numbers 32:23) Sin, then, is not primarily the violation of human laws. It is first and foremost the violation of the Divine Law; it is not primarily against our neighbor or society, it is against God.

It is precisely for this reason that the first four of the ten commandments have to do with our relationship to God, which is the supreme relationship, and the others (the second table) have to do with our relationship to fellowmen. Because we are created in the divine image, our first responsibility is to obey God.

Moreover, because God has commanded us to be in a right
relationship with Him by being in a harmonious relationship with
our neighbor. Thus, when we steal, commit adultery, lie or cheat
we offend not only our neighbor; we offend God. Sin, in the final
analysis, is always against God! This is why our LORD summed
up the Ten Commandments by urging his disciples:

> *"Thou shalt love the Lord thy God with all l thy heart, and with
> all thy soul ,and with all thy mind, and with all thy strength;
> this is the first commandment. And the second is like, namely
> this, Thou shalt love thy neighbor as thyself. There is none
> other commandment greater than this" (Mark 12:30-31).*

Let us ever bear in mind, that when we sin against our
fellowmen in any way whatsoever - gossip, cheating, stealing,
violating his/her rights - we sin against God.

"Against Thee, Thee only have I sinned and done this evil in
Thy sight" (vs 10).

Verses 7 - 8   Prayer for Cleansing (Reconciliation)

Continuing his great Prayer of Confession, after having humbly and unreservedly admitted his guilt, the Psalmist petitions the
God of mercy for cleansing. This prayer for cleansing marks a
major advance in his spiritual development. He is prepared not
only to admit that he has done wrong, what he desires now is to
be cleansed from sinfulness in order that he might grow spiritually. To put it more pointedly, in order that he might not commit
the same sin that he had done in the past.

Thus he prays:

> *"Create in me a clean heart, O God: and renew a right spirit
> within me."*

Confession is both negative and positive. Negatively, it calls
for the admission of guilt, of being willing to acknowledge that one
has done that which displeases God. Positively, it leads to

cleansing from those thoughts and words which lead to destructive actions.

More profoundly, confession is a therapeutic process. It is the means of healing the soul. Just as poison in an infected wound must be drained away or gotten rid of before healing can take place, so the soul must be purged of evil inclinations in order for the healing, brought about by confession, to take effect. Truly "confession, is good for the soul!"

Verse 10 - 17
Prayer for Restoration

The Psalmist continues. His prayer for cleansing is essentially the expression of his desire for the forgiveness of God. His great desire is for reconciliation. He has acknowledged that he has sinned and that this has created a breach between God and himself. It is this sense of estrangement from God which is the source of his sorrow. He desires to get back into a right relationship with His Maker.

David, a man after God's own heart, who had once enjoyed deep fellowship with God now finds himself "far from God." In confession he seeks to be again at one with God, and so he prays, "Cast me not away from thy presence" (11). What a prayer! Surely, every child of God desires to dwell continually in His Presence!

The desire of the Psalmist goes deeper. The element of confession runs through this Psalm very much like the theme in a great musical symphony. Again and again, the Psalmist admits his guilt and prays for the strength to amend his ways and to be reconciled to God. His consuming desire, however, is to engage in the praise of God. So, he cries: "O LORD, open thou my lips and my mouth shall shew forth thy praise" (vs 15).

Why does the Psalmist make this request? Why does he express the desire to praise the LORD? It is as we seek to answer these questions that we realize the essential relationship between

Confession and Praise in the process of prayer to Almighty God.

While conscious of his sinfulness, aware of his estrangement from God because of his sin, the Psalmist was deeply disturbed in spirit that he was unable to do that which he desired most - to praise the LORD. But, now having confessed his sin, and having been reconciled to God, he can burst forth into praise.

The example, then, of David, "a man after God's own heart" is most instructive to us when we think of the place of confession in prayer. When we have done wrong, when we know that we have broken the Divine Law, then let us go to God and confess to Him our sins. It does us no good to try to "cover- up" our sins. For, we do not go to God to inform Him of our sins. God already knows that we have transgressed! The omniscient Deity knows even before we come to Him that we have sinned! Let us, therefore, get it right!

We do not tell God anything new when we confess our sins to him (though it might be added, that often when we think that we are telling others something new, we are not!) Rather, what we do is to admit to God that we have done wrong. Concisely, we take responsibility for our actions. (The well known story of George Washington as a boy confessing that he had cut down a cherry tree is useful here. It would appear that his father, most likely, knew that he had done so. The important thing is that the boy "owned up" to having done this bad deed).

It is this willingness to take responsibility for our sinful actions which leads to cleansing and opens up the way for us to receive the forgiveness of God. It is precisely when this is realized that the greatness of David comes into sharp relief. It is easy to superficially enquire, "How can David be considered as a man after God's own heart when he abused his power by murdering and innocent man and committing adultery most blatantly?" The answer is that he can be considered in this righteous manner because he had the "guts" to admit his guilt before God and the humility to seek Divine forgiveness!

The path to perfection in the Christian life is not so much a continual advance to holiness, as a slow process with advances and set backs. Willingness of the person to admit his/her faults, "picking up the pieces" and moving on to greater achievements! So often it really means:

"Climbing   up   new   calvaries   ever....   "
It is, therefore, very significant that this great Prayer of Confession concludes: The sacrifices of God are a broken spirit, A broken and a contrite heart, O God, Thou will not despise. "

These words, coming out of a situation in which sacrifices were offered to God in seeking reconciliation after violation of the Divine Law, assures us that what the LORD desires is a "contrite heart." The assurance given here is that God, in His Divine mercy, is willing and anxious to receive and forgive the person who, having sinned, approaches Him humbly, confessing their guilt and seeking Divine Pardon. Indeed, is not this assurance the very heart of the Gospel?

If there is one theme which runs throughout the Bible "from cover to cover" it is this - God is love! It was out of this love for erring, rebellious mankind that God sent His Divine Son into the world. This is why St. Paul could say, "God was in Christ reconciling the world unto Himself." (2 Cor. 5:19). John proclaimed the essence of this Christian revelation in these immortal and challenging words:

" For God so loved the world that He gave His only begotten son, that whosoever believeth in him should not perish, but have everlasting life" (John 3:16).

Thus men and women in all ages, "from all walks of life," have turned to God in penitence, confessing their sins and have experienced the sublime joy of "forgiveness and reconciliation." Despite sinfulness, they have been ransomed, healed, restored, forgiven, and have continued their spiritual journeys, ever trusting in the God of their salvation.

And what of you, my friend? Are you burdened and "bogged down" by sin? Are there things which you have done in the past which still trouble your conscience? Are you among those who feel that the wrongs they have done in the past are such that they are unable to make spiritual progress? Is your relationship with God marred by sin? Is it your burning desire to be reconciled to your Maker? Is there something blocking your communion with God?

Then, the message of this chapter is for you! Be assured that if you approach God, offering the prayer of confession, acknowledging your sinfulness, and seeking His forgiveness, then you too will receive Divine forgiveness. You too will be reconciled to God. You will be forgiven and will be reconciled to God, the God who was in Christ reconciling the world unto himself. Come then, my brother, my sister, and with a humble, contrite heart, confess your sins to God.

> *"Let us, therefore, come boldly unto the throne of grace, that we may obtain mercy and find grace to help in time of need"* (Hebrews 4:16).

Confession then, is utterly essential for spiritual growth! Were when acknowledge past sins, we receive present forgiveness and are endowed with renewed strength for future spiritual warfare. As such, sincere prayer almost always involves a strong element of confession. Yes, "confession is always good for the soul!" It is also good for the body, mind and spirit.

> *"Jesus is seeking the wanderers yet, why do they roam? Love only waits to forgive and forget: Home! Weary wanderer, home! Wonderful love dwells in the heart of the Father above."* -Robert Walmsley

Exercises

1. What is confession?

2. Why is confession so necessary in prayer?

3. How can we improve our prayer life by the effective use of confession?

4. Think of a sin you have committed recently. Write a short prayer of confession seeking God's forgiveness.

5. "In confession we do not tell God anything about ourselves. We acknowledge to Him what we have done." (Discuss).

Message From the Wayside Pulpit
....Continue Steadfast in Prayer

The Wayside Pulpit" at Trinity Methodist Church, Frederick Street, is one of the most arresting sights in Nassau. Bahamians and tourists alike, in the thousands, everyday pass by the busy intersection where the stately church is located. There, right on the corner of Frederick Street and Trinity Place, is the "Wayside Pulpit," prominently displayed, giving a message with deep religious meaning to everyone who passes by.

The writer recalls that, on several occasions, the message of "The Wayside Pulpit" has come to him with particular relevance. Early in 1988, for instance, he was pierced to the heart by the message, which consisted of just four simple but very profound words:

Continue Steadfastly in Prayer

What an important message this is for us here! For, so often, we are inclined "to give up."

This is especially the case when we face the problem of unanswered prayer or when it is clear what we are praying for is not in accord with the will of God! Many confess that in such situations they have become discouraged and have not continued to be steadfast in prayer. Some even admit that they have given up prayer altogether as a result of such experiences!

Yet, if our prayer life is to be developed, we must continue "to be steadfast in prayer!" It is not enough to just pray "when we feel like it!" Nor should we just resort to prayer when we are in trouble! True, in such moments of our journey through this transitory life, we are in special need of God, and He is ever willing to hear our cry!

But prayer does require that we be consistent. We should continue to pray, not only when we are sick, but also when we are well, when everything seems to be "going our way" and all is well. Yes, in all the trials and tribulations as well as the moments of joy and triumph, it behooves us, as members of the Body of Christ, to turn to the LORD in prayer that He, by His grace may deliver us and keep us from going "the wrong way." Let us ever bear this in mind as we continue our journey through life.

Let us constantly turn to Him in prayer.

6

*P*RAYER

*I*S

*I*NTERCESSION

"Likewise the Spirit also helpeth our infirmities: for we know not what we should pray for as we ought: but the spirit itself maketh intercession for us with groanings which cannot be uttered. And he that searcheth the hearts knoweth what is the mind of the Spirit, because he maketh intercession for the saints according to the will of God (Romans 8: 26 - 27).

Samuel was displeased with the Israelites! This great man of God, who had been the judge, the spiritual and administrative leader of Israel for nearly forty years, was now faced with a major crisis of confidence! The Israelites came to him requesting that he make arrangements for them to have a king. Samuel found it hard to agree with this request on two grounds, one theological, the other personal.

Theologically, he held to the concept of the Kingship of God. He believed "with the old school" that there was no King of Israel other than Yahweh of Hosts. Indeed, this concept of kingship contrasted sharply to that which was held by the other nations of ancient times.

The kings of the pagan nations of antiquity were despots who ruled with an "iron hand." Samuel was not happy with the prospect of such a monarch ruling in "the land of God." Samuel believed that the Lord alone was the King and that the earthly ruler, was merely , "The Lord's executor!" The earthly monarch was there only to carry out the will of God and not to exercise the power over his subjects.

Samuel also regarded this as a personal slight. The Israelites were quite satisfied with his tenure as their administrative and spiritual ruler, exercising power as delegated by God. But his sons were not of the same high calibre as their father and the Israelites were worried about what might happen if they were called to exercise leadership. So, in a not-so-veiled criticism of the house of Samuel, they alleged that Samuel himself was becoming too old for the job and his sons were simply too corrupt to assume leadership (1 Samuel 8:4-5). It must have been a bitter pill for the old man to swallow! For, in calling for a king the Israelites were not only rejecting the ancient concept of God as the only King of Israel, they were also rejecting Samuel and his household!

What did Samuel do? His response was wise and compassionate, showing that to the end he was indeed a man of God "par excellence." He did not agree with their request. He must have felt, humanly speaking, very "down hearted." Despite this, he made just one promise to pray for them.

In an act of supreme graciousness, this old man, faced with a request from those whom he had served to the best of his ability for all his adult life, responded, "As for me, God forbid that I should sin against the LORD by ceasing to pray for you!" (1 Samuel 12:23).

The response of Samuel here is most exemplary. Although the Israelites had, in effect, rejected his advice and had criticized his sons, he still made it a point of duty to pray for them. Indeed, in so acting he foreshadowed the advice of the Master, "Pray for them who despitefully use you!" (Matthew 5:44)

Now, thus far in our study of prayer we have examined those aspects which have to do with our relationship with God. Since prayer is essentially communion with God, then it is only natural that we should bring our concerns to God. This is why we offer to God our praise, our thanks, bring to God our confessions and offer God thanks for His gifts to us.

But there is another very important aspect of prayer - our concern for others. There should always be an element of this concern for others in our prayer. Significantly, today there is more and more appreciation of the importance of intercession in prayer. Indeed, as our world becomes more and more of a "global village" we are made increasingly aware of the need of others, and our responsibility to offer prayer for them.

THE IMPORTANCE OF INTERCESSION

It is at once a great privilege and a major responsibility on the part of the Christian to offer prayer for others. It is a privilege because those who are in need of prayer want us to pray for them. Whether it be in the hospital ward, in an emergency of some kind or in a dangerous situation such as being in an airplane with engine trouble, people do welcome us when we offer to pray for them. I am sure that you have had the experience of meeting those who are not going to church, but who ask, "Pray for me!"

Often we answer in the affirmative and soon forget their request. But we should take them seriously! We should indeed remember them when we offer prayer during the service, counting it a joy to be able to pray for others. Yes, very seldom it is that a person refuses an offer to pray for him/her. Even the person who hardly ever darkens the door of a church or one who claims to be an atheist appreciates a word of prayer when facing some major crisis in life - sickness, the loss of a loved one, or pending danger which threatens life.

But not only is it a privilege to offer prayer for others more profoundly, it is a major responsibility of the Christian to offer prayer for others. As Christians, our prayer should never be selfish or self-centered. Rather, they should reflect our concern for the welfare of others.

Perhaps you have heard the story of the man who had a family of four including his wife and two children. Each evening he would pray: "God bless us four no more!

We may smile when we hear about this rather selfish gentleman, who cared only for his family (to his credit, he was a good family man!) However, so often our prayers are very similar to his - very self-centered and limited to our family and circle of friends. This, however, is not in keeping with the nature of the Christian faith which we profess. For when we reflect our faith, we cannot but come to the conclusion that the offering of intercessory prayer is our responsibility something which naturally flows from our existence as members of the Body of Christ.

The Biblical teaching about mankind is based upon the concept of its essentially corporate nature. This is well expressed in the divine comment upon Adam's lonely condition before the creation of Eve. "It is not good for man to be alone!" (Genesis 2:18). This concept is developed throughout the Bible, and it is emphasized that no one can realize his/her true potential apart from the tribe or group to which he/belongs. Thus, in the patriarchal narratives, especially those about Jacob and Esau and the Joseph, the individual is conceived of having identity and purpose only as part of the tribal grouping. The action of the one, then, is bound up with the destiny of the whole tribe and vice-versa! For example, the terrible sin of Achan brought calamity upon the whole nation (Joshua 7:1- 26).

The corporate nature of humanity developed fully in the history of Israel during the monarchy. A good king, who obeyed the teaching of Yahweh brought blessings and prosperity upon his people. On the other hand a bad king, who "caused Israel to sin" brought disaster and defeat upon his people. Indeed, the historical books, such as Kings and Chronicles, are all based upon this concept of the corporate nature of humanity, in which the destinies of monarchs and their subjects are entirely bound up one with the other.

Turning to the New Testament, this concept is developed in teaching about the Church. St. Paul teaches that the Church is the Body of Christ, and that the individual members make up this body. Their lives then touch each other and Christians are called upon to care for each other. Thus, St. Paul concludes his exhortation on the Church by declaring, "Now you are the Body of Christ and individually members of it" (1 Corinthians 12:27). As a member of the Body of Christ, the Christian has a deep and special relationship to others who belong to Christ, and as such, should continually offer prayer for those who belong "to the household of faith."

Our prayers of intercession, however, should not be limited to those who are members of the Church. Rather, they should be offered for all who are in need, whatever may be their color, race, condition, or creed. We need only reflect upon the ministry of our LORD Himself, in order to realize how essential it is for us to be concerned for the welfare of all those who are in need.

The motivating force, then, for our prayers of intercession must be love; not the fickle sentimental love which is based upon emotion, but that genuine love, agape, which is essentially a concern for the welfare and well being of others. The Bible has a lot to say about this special kind of love.

Indeed, at the heart of the Gospel is the message of Divine Love. The teaching of the Bible "from cover to cover" is that God is love. Its essential message is summed up by the apostle John in these immortal words:

"For God so loved the world that He gave His only Son, that whoever believed in Him should not perish but eternal life" (John 3:16 RSV).

The Ministry of the Divine Son, who came into the world to save sinners, was marked by the deep concern for the welfare of all, especially the outcasts of society, publicans, sinners "the wretched of the earth." Thus, at the beginning of His ministry, He defined his ministry:

"The Spirit of the Lord is upon me, because He has anointed me to preach good news to the poor. He has sent me to proclaim release to the captives and recovering of sight to the blind, to

set at liberty those who are opposed, to proclaim the accept-
able year of the LORD" (Luke 4:16 RSV).

Throughout his ministry, as recorded in the Gospels, He demonstrated this concern for the welfare of others. He healed the sick, gave sight to the blind, fed the hungry multitudes and even raised the dead.

In His prayers, He remembered those who were His disciples and who would come to believe in Him in ages to come (John 17). In His Sacrificial death upon the Cross of Calvary, He was "numbered among the transgressors," although He Himself committed no sin. By means of His death and resurrection, He wrought victory over sin and death for all who believed on Him. Truly, He can be described as "the man for others."

Since the Master cared so much for others, then we who are His disciples also ought to show love for those with whom we meet day by day. "This is the way the Master went, Must not His servants tread the same?"

Continuing our reflection on the theological basis of the prayer of intercession, we turn to the teaching of Jesus, where He is quite explicit on our responsibility to others. He summed up the teaching of the Law and the prophets by giving two great commandments:

"Thou shalt love the LORD thy God with all thy heart, and all thy soul and all thy might and Thou shalt love thy neighbor as thyself"

The first of these commandments has to do with our relationship to God, which, as we have seen is the supreme relationship which governs all others. When we think about the chapters we have covered thus far, we may note that, generally speaking, the first commandment is the basis of the aspects of prayer we have discussed thus far - praise, thanksgiving, petition and confession. Concisely, in offering praise to God, in making our petitions to God, in thanking God for benefits to us and in making confession to God we are indeed praying in accord with the commandment to love God with all the integrity we can.

Turning to the second commandment, we note that it has to do with our relationship to our neighbor, to the people we meet day by day. The Master commands that we should show love to them. And as we have seen, the Biblical understanding of love is most profound, calling upon us to exercise a genuine concern for the welfare of others. Thus, when we offer prayer for those who are in need, when we spend time upon our knees and make intercession for sinners, for the sick, for the bereaved, then we are praying in accord with the Second Great Commandment of the Master. This commandment gives theological backing for the offering of prayers of intercession.

It is clear, then, that there is a very sound Biblical and theological sanction for offering prayers for others. This three-fold theological basis of the prayer of intercession - the corporate nature of humanity, the vicarious nature of the Ministry of the Master and the Divine law of love - makes it obligatory for the Christian to include prayers for others in virtually all devotional exercises. Let us, then, explore this matter more deeply. What are the qualities which make for effective prayers of intercession?

SYMPATHY AND IDENTIFICATION

First, it can be confidently stated that if we are to be effective in our prayers of intercession, then we must be sensitive and alert to the needs of others. It requires a great degree of sympathy and identification with the needs of others to be able to offer prayers which will really meet their needs. Just as the Heavenly Father is sensitive to our needs, so must we be so near to others that we can sense their needs and offer the prayers which are most appropriate for them. There are many examples in Holy Scripture for us.

Think, for instance, of the call of Isaiah in the Temple. This passage, found in the sixth chapter of the Book of Isaiah, begins with an acknowledgment of the power, majesty and holiness of God. The young man has a vision of the LORD "high and lifted up" as the seraphim, with deep awe proclaim:

"Holy, holy, holy is the LORD of Hosts The fullness of the earth is His glory" (Isaiah 6:3).

The prophet's awareness of the holiness of God produces his consciousness of his own sinful condition.

But he is not alone. Rather, he is aware of the corporate nature of sin and identified with the nation. "Woe is me! For I am lost; for I am a man of unclean lips and I dwell in the midst of a people of unclean lips!" (Isaiah 6:5a,).

The prophet does not set himself from the sinful nation, but is deeply aware that he shares in its sinful condition. If we are to offer prayers of intercession which are effective, then we cannot set ourselves apart from society. We must be painfully aware of its failure and short comings, and in this way we can offer prayers which are relevant to its needs.

We must be constantly thinking about the ways in which others may be tempted to sin, and so pray for them. It is said of Job, that as a very good father there were times when he offered prayer for his children just in case they might have sinned. Job did not wait until his children had done something wrong and then rush to pray for them. (Job 1:5). Rather, he prayed for them continually so that they might be able to resist sin when tempted. (Job 1:5). He was a father who was deeply sensitive to the needs of his children!

SENSITIVITY

Sensitivity! This is required of us all. We must be always on the lookout, always alert so we can offer prayer and help for those in need.

A minister was doing his pastoral rounds in the hospital one evening. As he was leaving, having visited a number of patients, he saw two ladies standing on the steps of that institution. They were deeply worried. He enquired of them the reason for their worried looks. They explained that a gentleman who was very near and dear to them was very ill. He was the husband of the older lady and the father of the younger one, her daughter. The pastor visited the gentleman and had a word of prayer with him. It was because the pastor was alert and saw how worried the ladies were that he had the opportunity to minister to the needs of a very sick man who was deeply in need of prayer and most appreciative of them!

We must be alert and sensitive to the needs of others. We must constantly bear in mind that it is our Christian responsibility to pray for others. Like the Master Himself, we must be sensitive to the needs of others if we are to be effective in our prayers of intercession (Mark 6:34, John 17).

RESPONSIBILITY

Because it is our responsibility, our Christian duty to pray for others, we should do so whether they appreciate it or not. We should be persistent in offering prayer for them and continue to do so as long as we consider it necessary. This should depend, not on whether they are receptive to us, but on our sense of responsibility for them before God. Here we come up against one of the great prayers of intercession of the Bible - the Prayer of the righteous Abraham for the wicked cities of Sodom and Gomorrah. The story is recounted for us in the eighteenth chapter of Genesis.

It begins with a description of the cities of Sodom and Gomorrah. The inhabitants of these cities are described as being very wicked. Yet, in a strange way, their destinies are bound up with that of Abraham, whose righteousness and loyalty to God stand in stark contrast to the sinfulness of these people. Abraham's nephew Lot had chosen to dwell in the plains amongst the people of these cities. Their destruction is imminent!

The place of prayer for these cities is a hill overlooking them. Several of the men from the city have spoken to the patriarch. And now as they are about to return to these wicked places, the LORD reveals to Abraham that He is about to destroy them. Here on the mount overlooking the plains where Sodom and Gomorrah have sinned, Abraham begins to pray for their salvation. With great compassion and persistence he prays to the LORD for the sparing of the people of these cities.

What a moving scene! A great and righteous man prays for the saving of the people of two wicked cities. Like every true child of God, he takes no pleasure in the death of sinners! Yea, even as the outcry of the sins of the people in these cities rise to the heavens, the prayers of the righteous Abraham for the people arise to heaven pleading for the exercise of Divine mercy upon its erring inhabitants.

Thus, it is recorded, that Abraham approached God and asked, are you really going to destroy the innocent with the guilty? If there are fifty innocent people in the city, will you slay the whole city? Won't you spare it in order to save fifty? Surely you won't kill the innocent with the guilty. That's impossible! You can't do that! If you did that, the innocent would be punished with the guilty. That is impossible! The Judge of all the earth has to act justly (Genesis 18:22-25, GNB).

Abraham continued to plead for the saving of the people of these cities (Genesis 18:22-25 NEB). His persistence in pleading with God gradually led to a reduction of the number of innocent people required in order to save them. So, he continues, until he reaches the point where he asks, "Please don't be angry LORD, and I will speak just once more. What if only ten are found?" God Replied, "I will not destroy it if there are ten." (Genesis 18:26).

This is certainly an example of the prayer of intercession "par excellence." Here we see a great man of God pleading before the throne of mercy for the people of two cities who were corrupt to the core. Eventually, the cities are destroyed because not even ten innocent can be found in them. But it was not for want of prayer of intercession for them. They must have been very wicked cities indeed if so few righteous people could be found in them!

Now, it is quite clear from the context, that the evil inhabitants of these two cities did not request Abraham to pray for them! In fact, they were so depraved that they had forgotten God and abandoned any effort to conform to His moral law. It did not matter to them whether Abraham prayed for them or not!

Here the great spiritual power of Abraham shines! He offers

prayer persistent prayer for people who either could not or cared not to offer prayer for themselves. This is the very essence of intercession - a concern for others which is not based on our relationship to them but our understanding of their need. While the prayer of intercession is based on our relationship to others, it is our relationship to God which ultimately controls the way in which we should pray for others.

The wicked inhabitants of Sodom and Gomorrah had reached such a stage of depravity that it mattered not whether prayer was offered for them or not. Still Abraham prayed for them.

There is an extremely important lesson for us here. When we sense that people are in need of prayer, when we observe that they are going the wrong way, even when we are unable to stop them, and even when they make it clear that they really do not need or want us to pray for them, we should still continue to offer prayer for them! It is not for us to determine whether people appreciate our prayers or even to wonder whether they wish us to pray for them. What is important is our relationship to God. And if there are those who are in need of prayer, who might not really wish prayer, we should still offer prayer for them because the Master has commanded us to do so. It is our relationship to God which, in the final analysis, determines whether we ought to pray for others and not our attitude or relationship to them!

So, then, let us not worry about whether others wish us to pray for them. If they are in need of prayer, just let us pray for them! We must leave it to God to judge whether our prayers for them are in vain or whether they deserve the prayers offered on their behalf. Let us do our part and pray for them. Let us follow the example of Samuel who promised to pray for those who had rejected him. "As for me, God forbid that I should sin against the LORD in ceasing to pray for you!" (1 Sam 12:23)

We come now to consider the greatest prayer of intercession of all times..... the prayer of Jesus in the Garden of Gethsemane. Here, in this solitary place, the Master enters into deep communion with God. Known by many scholars as "The prayer of the Great High Priest," it is the longest prayer in the New Testament. It is devoutly recorded for us in the Seventeenth chapter of the Gospel according to St. John. Here "The Beloved Disciple" gives us a most intimate glimpse of the Master at prayer, allowing us to enter into "the holy of holies", the very mind of Christ as he prays for His disciples, for the Church and for the World. Here we see Jesus, the Saviour of the world, in deep spiritual agony as he offers this powerful and most comprehensive prayer of intercession.

This prayer falls naturally into three distinct parts:

The Invocation

Jesus' relationship to God.   Ver. 1-5.

Jesus' Prayer for His Disciples.   Ver. 6-19.

Jesus' Prayer Church and the World.   Ver. 20-26.

Let us examine each section carefully -

1) JESUS' RELATIONSHIP TO GOD - VER. 1-5: Jesus begins by addressing God in that special way which was His because of His relationship to God as the Divine Son - "Father." As has been pointed out, Jesus addressed God in this way, using the expression that a child of His times would instinctively speak to his/her earthly father. Not only did Jesus begin His own prayer in this way; he also taught His disciples to begin their own petitions by calling God, "Our Father." He prays, that as He completes his mission on earth He may be glorified. His mission - he realizes that His own mission is being fulfilled - is that He might be the Means for the giving of eternal life to all mankind.

He defines eternal life thus: "This is eternal life; to know thee who alone art truly God, and Jesus Christ, whom thou has sent" (John 17:3, NEB).

Jesus then, begins with an invocation which places His relationship to God in true perspective. In the context of this unique relationship, He expresses His satisfaction that His ministry is in line with the will of His Heavenly Father - the granting of eternal life to all who believe in His Divine Sonship.

2) THE PRAYER FOR THE DISCIPLES - VER. 6-19 Jesus now

prays for His disciples. He continues: "I pray for them. I am not praying for the world, but for those you have given me, for they are yours."

It is most significant to observe that Jesus offered prayers for His disciples immediately after His invocation to His Heavenly Father. He had called them out of the world to be with Him and to continue His ministry by preaching, teaching and healing the sick, both mentally and physically (Mark 3:13-17, Luke 9:1-6). They had been with him throughout His ministry and now in the hour of persecution, they were especially in need of prayer. For, it is recorded that even as He was praying, there was one of the disciples who was plotting to betray Him to the religious authorities. (John 18:1-9). And soon, one of the most faithful and outspoken, Simon Peter, would deny that He ever knew Him. (Matthew 26:69- 3). Indeed, it is recorded that when the soldiers came to arrest Him "they all forsook Him and fled." The disciples of Jesus, in this crucial hour, on the night in which He was betrayed, on the eve of the Crucifixion, were in special need of prayer!

3) JESUS PRAYS FOR THE CHURCH - VER. 6-28 In the third part of this great prayer, Jesus, brings before the Throne of Grace, the Church. It is true that the disciples failed the Master in this time of great testing. Yet, it is noteworthy that he expresses great confidence in them. He believes that their ministry would bear fruit. Thus He prays confidently "My prayer is not for them alone. I pray for those who will believe in me through their message" (John 17-20 NIV).

Jesus, then, peering down through the centuries, prophetically prays for the Church in all ages. He prays that those who would believe on Him would be united. But His prayer is wider; it covers the world. His prayer is that Christians might be united in their witness to the world. Ultimately, the purpose of the mission of Christ and His Church, in all ages, are one and the same - the gift of eternal life, which is salvation, to all mankind!

As we examine this prayer of intercession of Our LORD, we

realize that it is the model we should follow in our own prayers offered for others.

Note that he begins with an Invocation and in communion with His Heavenly Father. He establishes His relationship with God before He offers prayer for others. This is an extremely important lesson for us in our own prayer life.

We should get our relationship with God in proper perspective FIRST, and then offer prayers for others. Praise, petitions to God, confession and thanksgiving for God's gifts to us, should take place before intercession. Concisely, we cannot pray effectively for others unless we first enter into a right relationship with God. This is precisely why the Bible declares that, "The prayer of the righteous availeth much" (James 5:16).

Here we have a striking parallel to our own witness as Christians. It has been demonstrated in history and through experience that the Christian must first receive the saving grace of God in Christ before he/she can witness to others. John Wesley was not able to witness effectively to the world until he had his own conversion experience in which he testified, "I felt my heart strangely warmed." Just as we must first receive a right relationship with God in prayer before we can pray effectively for the needs of others.

Let us, then, reflect on the pattern that we should follow in our own prayers.

First we begin with our relationship with God. We praise God, thank Him, make our petitions to Him and confess to Him where we have sinned and seek His forgiveness.

Thus, ransomed, healed, restored and forgiven, we are ready to offer prayer for the needs of others.

Secondly, then, we remember before God those who are nearest and dearest to us. We pray for the members of our household - our parents, wives and children, and any others who are with us. We think of those who are members of our family and who are away from home - a child at school, a relative on holiday, a member of the family who is in the hospital. Continuing, we offer prayer especially for any of our household who are sick and we think of relatives and friends who may be worried. Here, we should think especially of any elderly members of our family who are in a hospital or nursing home.

Thirdly, we think of the household of faith - the Church. We note that Jesus prayed for His disciples, those who like ourselves, are seeking to follow Christ.

Let us at this stage, remember before God the members of the congregation of the local Church to which we belong. Many of our Churches have weekly bulletins with lists of members who are ill, or abroad, or in any special need. We should use this bulletin regularly and not just for news, but as a means of praying for those in need.

Then, we should bear up before God one who is always in need of our prayer - our pastor. We often ask him to pray for us, but do we pray for him/her? Surely, your pastor, as he goes about his pastoral duties and meets the demands of our times, does need your prayer. Indeed, every pastor will testify that they are greatly assisted and encouraged in his/her ministry by the assurance that there are members of the congregation who remember their pastors in their prayers. Yes, do remember to pray for your pastor!

Having prayed for the Church, we should extend our prayer concerns to the wider community. We should pray for the nation in which we live and especially remember its leaders, both temporal and spiritual. The words of the First Epistle to Timothy are most instructive:

"First of all, I urge that petitions, prayers and intercessions, and thanksgivings be offered for all men; for sovereigns and all in high office, that we may lead a tranquil and quiet life in full observance of religion and high standards of morality. Such prayer is right, and approved by God our Saviour, whose will it is that all men should find salvation and come to know the truth" (1 Tim. 2:1-2 NEB).

It is extremely important that we should be aware of the major concerns of those who are in authority in our nation. Our prayers of intercession would be greatly enriched as we keep before us our daily newspaper.

Continuing, we should offer prayer for the whole community of mankind. Here we should be especially aware of the mission of the Church to the world. We can pray for the world, confident that in the end Christ will triumph over the forces of evil.

THE PRAYER OF INTERCESSION REQUIRES COMPASSION

Then, if we are to pray effectively for those who are in need of prayer, we must exercise compassion, [or as we are led to exercise compassion]. Compassion, as we know, leads to action for the welfare of others; it is not just "feeling sorry for them." It means being identified with them and, as a result, doing something concrete to improve their situation.

As we examine the Ministry of the Master, we understand the meaning of compassion. We are told that when the multitudes came to Him in a desert place, they were hungry. The Master had compassion upon them as He knew of their condition. This led him to perform the great miracles of the feeding of the multitudes. His compassion upon them, and His offering of prayer for them, resulted in action to relieve their hungry situation by the provision of bread for their needs.

Likewise, as we offer prayers of intercession today for others, we are led to do something positive to relieve their condition. There are many who testify that as a result of praying for a person with a particular need, they were moved to do something positive to help the condition of that person! Perhaps, we can all think of cases where our praying for someone moved us to positive action. Indeed, prayer ushers in action. In a sense most profound, intercession forms the link between "the world of work" and the "world of prayer." Intercession is all embracing and comprehensive in nature. In the prayer of intercession we join with the LORD in prayer for the benefit of another.

The inclusion of intercession, then, adds variety, freshness and vigor to our prayer life! As we begin to reflect upon the needs of our family, the Church and the world in general, we soon realize that there is no end to the number of concerns that we can bring before the Throne of Grace. Following the example of the Master, beginning with our own relationship to God, we can go on to pray for our family, for the Church and for the world.

In our age, in which there is such a great concentration on "the search for meaning," it is easy for us to become so caught up in our relation with God, our petitions, our wants and our needs that we forget the needs of others who are around us. However, if we are to grow in our prayer life, then, we must continually bear others in mind as we come to God. We must exercise a true priestly ministry in ever seeking to bring to the Throne of Grace those who are in need of prayer. Religious leaders of mankind in all ages - saints such as Polycarp, Augustine of Hippo, Francis of Assisi, Wesley, Luther, Mary Slessor of Calabar, G. Campbell Morgan, and Mother Theresa of our own day - have constantly been deeply conscious of the needs of their fellow human beings, whom they consistently commended in their prayers.

Indeed, there are those in every age who feel that they have been called to a special ministry - offering prayer of intercession. Thus one contemporary religious leader has established a world-wide ministry of intercession. Moreover, the world famous evangelist, Billy Graham, tells us that one of his daughters spends literally hours on her knees every morning. Why? Because she has a deep conviction that she has been called by God to exercise a ministry of intercession.

Thus, in offering the prayer of intercession, in participating in this truly priestly method of ministry, we are, indeed, "treading where the saints have trod," and are treading!

As we offer the prayer of intercession, we come to realize , that, in so doing, our own spiritual life is greatly strengthened and enriched. We develop to the point where, as we grow spiritually, we cannot pray without thinking of others! Indeed, we find that our prayer life is incomplete unless we are prepared to offer prayer for others. Concisely, we are not satisfied to receive our blessing in prayer unless, by means of intercession, we become the source of the blessing for others. As the spiritual heirs of Abraham, our prayer is that we may become a means of great blessing and so grow in our own spiritual strength.

The offering of intercession is, in a sense, most profound in our prayer life and the spiritual expression of one of the greatest of the virtues which the Master bids us practice - mercy. It was Shakespeare who said: "The quality of mercy is twice blessed. It blesses him that gives and him that takes." So, is the quality of the prayer of intercession!

The prayer of intercession is twice blessed! It blesses the one for whom prayer is offered. It is, indeed, such a great source of comfort to know that there are those who are praying for us! Even the most hardened of persons, even those who admittedly are not deeply religious, even those who claim to be atheists, are still comforted to know that "someone is praying for me." Indeed, very seldom does anyone ever refuse the offer of prayers. Thus the prayer of intercession is a deep and wide source of blessing as prayers are offered for the nation, for society and for those in need.

But, not only is it a source of blessing for those for whom prayer is offered. The prayer of intercession also blesses the one who prays!

As we offer prayers of intercession, we are lifted from the bonds of our narrow concerns and interests, of our problems and trials to consider the needs of others. So often when we think about our own problems, we imagine that they are the greatest in the world. When our bills are high and our cash low, when we feel that we are "not in the best of health," when we are tempted to engage in self-pity, as we reflect upon the needs of others we realize that our problems pale in comparison with what others have to "put up with."

At such times, it behooves us as Christians to offer prayer for those who are in need. We should be people "standing in the gap" praying like Abraham, for the wicked and wayward, like Moses for those who are backsliding, in their faith and ministry, praying like our LORD Himself, for the unity of His people here on earth. For it is as we lift our hearts in prayer to God for others, that we realize how great is their need and how necessary it is for us to offer prayer for them, and do what we can, by the grace of God to relieve their condition.

Thus, as we pray in this way, we realize that spiritual power is being made available for the benefit of others. It is by nature, deeply satisfying. Thus, we arise from offering prayer for others, exhausted and drained, but at the same time, deeply satisfied and joyful in the assurance that we have contributed to the well being of another child of God! Following the example of the Master, let us continually offer prayer for the welfare of the members of our families and our friends, for the edification of our fellow members of the Body of Christ, and, indeed, for all who dwell upon "this celestial ball," in which "we live and move and have our being!"

OFFERING PRAYERS
OF INTERCESSION

"The effectual fervent prayer of a righteous man availeth much"   (James 5:16).

OUR EXAMPLE: THE MASTER AT PRAYER. John 17

STRUCTURE

I. INVOCATION Acknowledgment of the greatness of God. (Praise) May also include the acknowledgment of the goodness of God. (Thanksgiving) Acknowledgment of the graciousness of God. (Petition) Acknowledgment of the mercy of God. (Confession).

PRAYERS OF INTERCESSION

1. THE FAMILY. Immediate family circle, "Us four no more." Family of orientation, family of procreation. Spouse, children, grand children. Parents, brothers, sisters. Extended family - cousins, uncles, aunts, in-laws. Members of household. Close friends.

2. "THE HOUSEHOLD OF FAITH. Sick and "shut in" members

of one's local congregation. Members of officers. The Pastors of one local congregation. Church leaders and officers - bishops, clergy, deacons, elders, etc. Laypersons in the Church. The youth ministry of our Church. The mission of the Church. Those who are serving abroad.

3. PERSONS WITH SPECIAL NEEDS. Those who are sick and suffering, especially any known to us. People suffering from certain diseases of the body - cancer, heart disease, diabetes, and most pertinently at this time, AIDS. People suffering from disorders of the mind. Couples whose marriages are "on the rocks." Persons who work in dangerous occupations. People involved in education of the youth. People known to us who are undergoing great stress and anxiety in their lives. People faced with crucial decisions affecting their future - important exams, job interviews etc.

4. OUR COMMUNITY/NATION Those in positions of authority in the state - the head of state, Ministers of Government, civil servants, judges and those who maintain the law. Those who are in the helping professions - doctors, nurses, hospital workers. Those in the field of education. Youth leaders and people who give their time and energy in serving the needy in our community. People known to us who are engaged in community service, especially those who serve on a voluntary basis. Those who are especially concerned for the preservation of the earth's treasures, the creation of our Bountiful God.

5. THE WORLD The leaders of the nations of the world. The office of the United Nations. Those who are engaged in efforts to bring about peace and justice in the world. People known to us who are in positions of authority and influence in the world. Those who suffer persecution because of their faith. The ecumenical movement and those involved in it. Those who are engaged in dialogue with believers of other faiths. Those engaged in rescue work at the international level. Those engaged in steps to bring about reconciliation between warring parties/nations. Those engaged in the fight for justice.

6. OUR ENEMIES. "Pray for those who despitefully use you."

Here, let us bring before the throne of grace any person whom we regard as an enemy, those who have been hostile unforgiving, or unkind to us. Pray for your enemies and they may become your friends.

7. PRAYERS FOR THE CONVERSION OF SINNERS. A special time of prayer should be reserved for those who are in need of salvation. We should be constantly offering prayers of intercession that more people may turn from their sins and find the grace of God available to them. There is a variety of subjects to offer prayers of intercession for, therefore, we must continually offer prayer for others.

THE FAMILY

THE HOUSEHOLD OF FAITH

PERSONS WITH SPECIAL NEEDS

THE COMMUNITY / NATION

THE WORLD

OUR ENEMIES

THE CONVERSION OF SINNERS

A PRAYER FOR RECONCILIATION

We live in an age in which there are great pressures upon the institution of marriage. There is a high divorce rate in many countries. Many couples experience major difficulties in keeping their marriages fresh, pure and meaningful over a long period. Often, they turn to the Church for help. As such, an important ministry of the Church today is marriage counselling. An integral part of this ministry is prayer for those with marital problems.

Here is a prayer to be used especially for those who are facing such difficulties yet desire their marriage to be successful and happy:

O LORD, BEHOLD THIS COUPLE! WHOSE MARRIAGE IS "ON THE ROCKS." ONCE THEY WERE HAPPY TOGETHER: BUT TODAY THEY ARE NOT HAPPY. ONCE THEY LIVED IN PEACE AND HARMONY BUT NOW THEIR RELATIONSHIP IS MARRED BY DISHARMONY. ONCE THEY DID THINGS TOGETHER. BUT TODAY THEY DO EVERYTHING SEPARATELY. ONCE THEY ADMIRED AND CARED FOR EACH OTHER. NOW THEY DO NOT CARE FOR EACH OTHER. ONCE THEY HAD A SPARKLE AND GLOW IN THEIR RELATIONSHIP. BUT NOW IT HAS GONE SOUR AND THEY QUARREL ALL THE TIME.

YET, O LORD, THEY WANT TO BE TOGETHER! THEY WANT THEIR MARRIAGE TO WORK. HEAL THEIR MARRIAGE! HELP THEM TO LOVE EACH OTHER AGAIN. RESTORE TO THEM THAT DEEP PURE LOVE OF THEIR EARLY DAYS TOGETHER.

YOU WHO BLESSED THE MARRIAGE FEAST AT CANA, SANCTIFY THIS MARRIAGE WITH THY PRESENCE. O THOU WHO HAST TAUGHT US THAT - "LOVE FULFILLS THE LAW" AND "WHO, FOR THE LOVE OF MANKIND, DID SEND YOUR DIVINE SON INTO THE WORLD," ENABLE THIS ESTRANGED COUPLE TO LOVE EACH OTHER AGAIN THAT THEY MAY CONTINUE IN YOUR DIVINE LOVE UNTIL THEIR LIVES END. BLESS THEM AND KEEP THEM TOGETHER IN THE BONDS OF MATRIMONIAL LOVE THROUGH JESUS CHRIST WE PRAY." AMEN.

7

PRAYER

IS

LISTENING

"....and the LORD remembered her." (1 Samuel 1:19)

"But the LORD was wroth with me for your sake, and would not hear me: and the LORD said unto me, Let it suffice thee; speak no more unto me of this matter" (Deut. 3:26).

"My grace is sufficient for you..." (11 Corinthians 12:10).

"...O, my Father, if it be possible, let this cup pass from me; nevertheless, not as I will, but as thou wilt" (Matthew 26:39).

Does God answer prayer? Will God answer my prayer? Does God, the mighty Creator of the whole universe, care for me? Will you pray for me?

Questions such as these are addressed to us daily. People really want to know whether their prayers are answered. With their concerns, their worries, their cares and so many problems, they wonder whether God is really One who cares for them. Indeed, throughout the ages, questions on the nature of prayer have been asked of Christians.

Today, as we think of our own world, these questions are most relevant. For, we live in times when the whole matter of prayer is being contested. There are those who wonder whether God can really make a difference in the affairs of mankind. Many seem to have a concept of a God who created the universe and has left it to mankind to "run its affairs." In this age of high technology and so many human achievements, the question of the nature of prayer is most urgent. As such, it is most appropriate that we should once again engage in the most profound question with regard to prayer. We must ask, in all sincerity, "Does God answer prayer?"

I recall that when I was a child, I used to visit an old aunt. She was a very devout Christian who had a number of Christian signs and bulletin boards in the house.. One of these read: "Every prayer is answered in God's way." Over the years, these words have never left me. I do not recall who wrote them or where she obtained this arresting and meaningful poster. All I know is that its message is very real, in that it affirmed, in all clarity that God does answer prayer.

This is certainly in keeping with the teaching of the Bible about God. If there is one thing that is clear, it is that God is a personal God, whose ears are open to the cries of mankind.

Thus, it was when Abraham prayed to God for the wicked cities of Sodom and Gomorrah, the LORD responded. And although there was eventual destruction because there was not found enough righteous people in those cities to redeem them from impending doom, it is clear from the Scriptures that God was willing to give Abraham a hearing (Genesis 18:18-33). Again, the LORD heard the cry of the Israelites when in bondage in Egypt, and delivered them through the marvelous ministry of Moses His servant (Exodus 3:1-12; 14-15). Moreover, Moses approached God, on several occasions, deeply convinced that He was a God who would hear, those ears were open to the cries of His people. The great prophet Elijah, in the encounter on Mount Carmel prayed to God believing that he would answer in a dramatic display of His power over the pagan Gods which, through the influence of Jezebel, were worshipped by many in Israel (I King 18). And, Jesus in the Prayer of the Great High Priest, offered intercession for Christians in all ages (John 17).

These examples all give clear testimony to the fact that the Biblical understanding of God is that He is a personal God who hears the cries of mankind. Unlike the idol gods of wood and stone, who have eyes to see and do not see and ears to hear and do not hear not." He is the God whose ears are ever open to the cries of mankind.

It is the testimony of Scripture that the God revealed in Christ as Divine Love, answers the prayers of those who come to Him in sincerity. But how does God answer prayer? Is it always in the affirmative? Does he sometimes simply tell us "No?" It is to answer these perplexing but most urgent questions that this chapter is devoted.

1. WHEN GOD ANSWERS "YES"

There are times, blessed times, when the answer of God to our prayer is clearly and unequivocally "Yes!" Take, for instance, the case of Hannah. As we have seen, she earnestly prayed to God for a son and her petition was granted. In the King James Version it is recorded that "The Lord remembered her." (1 Sam. 1:119). In Biblical teaching, when God "remembers" someone it is a sign of divine blessing, of granting a special request or helping him/her in a very special way.

The Bible teaches that God does answer prayer! There are instances from the Old and New Testaments which clearly show that God answers prayer. But the question which no doubt arises is, "DOES HE ANSWER PRAYER TODAY?" This is a burning issue for contemporary practical man.

It should be noted that throughout the ages, Christians have come to realize and experience that God does answer prayer positively! Likewise, He answers prayer today. Listen, for instance, to the testimony of a young lady, whose son was born with a defective heart.

Our God is a good and wonderful God. Can He still work miracles? We shall see from the following story what kind of God we serve. Mrs Onis Sinclair relates her testimony:

"It all started on March 8, 1978, when a baby boy of 6 pounds 5 ozs. as born to Mr. & Mrs. Onis Sinclair at the Princess Margaret Hospital in Nassau.

From day one the baby was like a crying cymbal. He was baptized at the Ebenezer Manse and the minister, the Rev. Patterson Deane remarked that "boys will be boys" when the baby cried persistently. However, I knew differently.

No one was aware of his illness, but his constant cries gave everyone great concern. He was bluish in color and his feet were so swollen that it felt like you could pick his toes off.

On his four-week check-up, the examining doctor gave me a start. She jumped back frightfully when she sounded his heart. I asked if anything was wrong, but she gently said I should go to the front desk and ask the nurse to make an appointment to see Dr. Maud Stevenson at her clinic at the Princess Margaret Hospital on Friday of that same week. I could not wait to get to the clinic as I did not know what to expect. The baby continued his cries and sleepless days and nights as I waited for 1 o'clock Friday to come.

We arrived to the clinic on time, only to find out that it was the Heart Clinic where children with heart disorders are brought. I was scared. Dr. Stevenson was beautiful. She was also gentle, kind and reassuring.

On examining Hansen, she told me that he had a heart problem, but it could be corrected. I got his medication and left the hospital.

My job now was to bring the news to my husband when he returned to Nassau. He believes in me and whatever I tell him would not make a difference in his attitude towards me and the child. When I caught him in a good mood, I told him what the doctor had said. He accepted the explanation without reservation.

My main task had now begun. For the first year of his life, Hansen lived in and out of the hospital. He never stayed at home for more than four weeks at any one time.I lost my job after he was born, but I accepted it as part of God's plan, because He knew that I could not go to work with the way Hansen was.

On April 3, 1979, Hansen was admitted to Jackson Memorial Hospital for tests and possible surgery. His first surgery was done the following day, when a portion of his liver was used to patch a hole in the aorta. He returned to Nassau five days later, a more relaxed baby who would now sleep at nights and take his food.

In August of that year, he took his first baby step. I rejoiced as I knew God was with me and that there was hope. I prayed night and day for God to help me to handle the situation in the best way possible. He did. I returned to work that same summer.

Hansen made good progress since the first operation and his hospital visits decreased from weekly to monthly, to quarterly to half yearly. He entered school at age six. I informed his teacher of his condition and ask her to look for symptoms - like bluish discoloration, shortness of breath, drowsiness, nausea and fainting. Should he experience any of these, I told her, she should call me as he would be running into difficulty and must be taken to the hospital immediately. She understood and promised to notify me of any changes.

On September 24, 1984, the day "the eye" of hurricane David was over Nassau, I had to take Hansen to Jackson Memorial Hospital because he was experiencing great difficulty in almost all the areas mentioned above. He was admitted to the Hospital that night, so I returned to Nassau the following day, only to find out that my father had passed away the day before, the same day I took Hansen to Jackson Memorial Hospital. Without losing any time, I grabbed Donna and Onissa and prepared to leave Nassau for Jamaica the following day. My husband was at sea.

My father was buried October 4, 1984 and Hansen had the second surgery on October 6, with correction being done to the auricles. He returned to Nassau on October 16 and continued at school as usual.

Since the second operation, his hospital visits remained at twice yearly and his health had greatly improved. The doctors advised me that he needed a third and final surgery, but they were being cautious as they anticipated an all-day procedure. They said that he had combined every possible heart disorder that anyone could think of and more!

In August of 1988, the doctors finally agreed to have surgery again. Hansen was admitted to Jackson Memorial Hospital on September 4 for surgery on the 8th. Can God still work miracles? Yes, He can!

Hundreds of prayers were offered on Hansen's behalf, before and during surgery. Instead of an all-day tiring surgery, all was done in two and a half hours! Miraculous, isn't it? My God is able and from Hansen's illness, I've come to trust Him more each day.

For the first time in his life, Hansen was able to walk without fainting or tiring. He did not win a trophy at Omnifest '88, but he is a winner as he successfully completed the mile on January 28, 1989.

I believe God chose me to look after this boy, soon to be 11 years old. During his illness, I was never put down, but I tried my best to encourage him on. From the day I found out what Hansen's illness was, I knew I had to be strong, devoted, patient, dedicated, caring and understanding to his cause. From the doctors first report on Hansen's condition, I knew I had to trust God for sustenance and guidance during this ordeal.

My thanks to all of you who prayed with me and for me, and a special "Thank you" to God for choosing me to mother this boy. Thanks too, to the Sassoon Heart Association, who stood by me all the way."

To you out there, I would say - "With God, all things are possible." His true greatness can reflect in your lives and in any circumstances.

Maybe He has chosen you to tackle a difficult task, just to test your faith in Him. Hold on, just let God have His way. Yes, God does answer prayers! He is still a miracle-working God! His ears are still open to the cries of all who call upon Him in sincerity. This is precisely why we can approach His throne boldly with our petitions. Since we are coming to the King of kings and the LORD of lords, we can afford to bring big and bold petitions with us to the Throne of Grace.

II WHEN GOD SAYS "NO!"

Because He is a powerful God and Sovereign Lord over the universe, He does not always answer in the affirmative. Sometimes, His answer is just the opposite, "No!"

Take Moses for instance. In the final days of his earthly sojourn, having led the Israelites literally to the border of the Promised Land, the very banks of the River Jordan, the great patriarch had one burning desire - to enter the Promised Land. He desired more than anything else to cross the Jordan and to spend his last days in the Promised Land. But it was denied him. Just think of it! Moses had led the children of Israel out of Egypt, their home of bondage. MOSES HAD, BY THE GRACE OF GOD, PERFORMED MIRACLES BEFORE THEM IN THE WILDERNESS. MOSES HAD BEEN THE DIVINELY APPOINTED MEDIATOR OF THE COVENANT AND LAW (Exodus 19-20).

Yet, when Moses, a man who was so close to God that it is said that he conversed with God "as a man with his friend," prayed earnestly that he cross the Jordan, God flatly rejected his request. God's answer, acidly expressed in Deuteronomy is: "LET IT SUFFICE THEE, speak no more to me of this matter" Deuteronomy 3:19.

In other words, God was telling Moses that "You have done your part. Moses, be content." God directed him to Joshua. The divine response was clear - Moses was not to cross Jordan, it was only his responsibility to designate another to do so. Thus, the great patriarch was translated, with his fondest desire denied!

Yes, my dear friends, there are times when God says "NO!" to us. There may be things that we desire greatly. But God may intervene and change our plans.

Dr. Thomas Coke was the great pioneer of the missionary endeavors of Methodism. Short in stature, like the Biblical Zaccheus, he was nevertheless a dynamo who always sought to proclaim the Gospel in far away places. He accomplished a tremendous amount of missionary work covering an amazing amount of territory by land and sea, before the jet age!

Thus in 1784 he, along with Asbury, was instrumental in establishing Methodism in America. Christmas day 1786 found him in Antigua, kindling the flame of Methodism already lit by that illustrious layman Nathaniel Gilbert. In 1789 he was in Jamaica, where he also established Methodism.

Coke, however, had a consuming desire to spread the message of Methodism (the saving grace of God in Christ) to the peoples of the Far East. He desired to serve in India and Ceylon. So, he set sail for the Far East. He never made it. He died and was buried at sea. Coke had finished his task and when he would go further afield, God intervened and effectively stopped him.

God does say no in various ways. The great Scots New Testament scholar William Barclay, in one of his commentaries has this solemn word to say "We would save ourselves a lot of worry if we realized that certain things were not for us." This is so true. There are times when God says "NO." We would, indeed, save ourselves much unnecessary worry (and ulcers!) if we realize when God is saying "NO" to us and govern ourselves accordingly! May we pray:

> *God grant me the courage to   change the things I can.*
> *The grace to accept the things I cannot.*
> *And the wisdom to   know the difference.*

III "WAIT!!!"

Sometimes the answer of God is "Yes." Sometimes it is "No." But oftentimes, the answer of God to our prayer is not immediately clear. In such situations, there is only one stance we can take "Wait!"

When the sisters of Lazarus sent an urgent message to Jesus requesting Him to come immediately because their brother was ill, the Lord did not rush to the scene! Rather He waited for a few days at a village which was far away from Bethany. By the time He got to Bethany, Lazarus was dead and buried.

Martha, the action-oriented sister of the dead disciple met Jesus and mildly rebuked Him for being so long. With remorse and sorrow, she rasped. "If you had been here, Sir, my brother would not have died!" (John 11:25). Martha, who was always anxious to see action and "to get things done," could not understand why Jesus did not come immediately when He was called upon by the distressed sisters. But there was a reason for the delay of the Master. It was implicit in His words to the disciples when first summoned, "this illness will not end in death; it has come for the Glory of God; to being glory to the Son of God" (John 11:4).

And so it was that Jesus performed the greatest of His miracles, or as John prefers to call them, "Signs" - the raising of Lazarus from the dead. In the process, He proclaimed the great hope which is at the heart of the Gospel, one which has brought comfort to countless millions of distressed over the centuries, in the face of death, "I am the resurrection and the life, he that believeth in me shall never die" (John 11:25).

Martha and Mary, the sisters of Lazarus had to learn that the Lord does not always work according to human time tables. They were anxious for Him to come to the rescue of their sick brother. He came in His time and accomplished more than they could ever expect. He raised their brother from the dead and in so doing demonstrated that the Gospel speaks of a Power which conquers even death and brings hope to the bereaved.

"WAIT! WAIT! WAIT!!!" This is a message which the Bible proclaims so often as it teaches us about prayer. It is a lesson which modern man has to learn over and over again, for ours is an age of speed and of instant action. We are constantly trying to find "short cuts" and to produce instant products. We find it hard to be patient. Yet, if we are to develop our prayer life, we must learn to wait.

In Biblical teaching, "waiting" is not merely resignation. Rather, it is waiting expectantly. It is epitomized in that watchful attitude which humbly and confidently waits upon God. It is by no means resignation. Rather it is EXPECTATION WITH CONFIDENCE. So, Moses exhorted the Israelites at the Red Sea to wait and see what the LORD would do for them. Moses knew that God would intervene to assist the Israelites. They only had to wait for His instructions.

In St. Luke there were those who were waiting. Such were Zacharias and Elizabeth, the pious parents of John who were waiting for the coming of the Messiah. The answer to God is not always immediate. Let us learn this. Often God's answer is wait. The Psalmist sums it up well: "Wait on the LORD. Be of good courage, Wait, I say, on the LORD!"

IV WHEN THE ANSWER IS "GROW!"

While there are times when the answer of God is very clear or when He advises us to be patient, there are also times when His answer is entirely different. At such times it is the intention of God to teach us a lesson of great meaning for our spiritual development. Concisely, in such situations, the answer of God is highly instructive, "GROW!"

Take for instance the case of St. Paul. His experience was different from that of Moses or Hannah. The great Apostle confesses that he suffered from an illness which caused him great physical pain. So hurtful did he find this malady, that he called it "a messenger from Satan." While scholars over the many centuries of study of the text, have made various suggestions (an eye disease, malaria, etc.), we really do not know precisely what it was as Paul never tells us. All we do know is that it caused him a great amount of suffering. So great was his suffering from this disease, that Paul testifies that ON THREE OCCASIONS, he earnestly prayed to God for healing. But St. Paul was not healed of this disease. Does it mean that God had not answered his prayer? By no means.

The answer of God is to be found in those most profound words from II Corinthians "MY GRACE IS SUFFICIENT FOR YOU: FOR MY STRENGTH IS MADE PERFECT IN WEAKNESS."

No, God did not heal Paul's disease. Rather he assured the apostle that His grace was sufficient to keep him. He did not need healing. All he needed was the assurance that the LORD was with him and teaching him. So, it was that through this experience St. Paul improved in his own spiritual life. He realized that it is often in our own human illness that we learn to depend on the Strength and power of God.

It may be that God is not answering your prayer in the way that you expect. But He may be speaking to you in order that your spiritual life may be deepened. There is nothing more satisfying to the soul than sincere and heartfelt prayer. It is as we pray that we develop spiritually, and by the grace of God come to the measure of the fullness of the stature of Christ.

Let us remember always that the Christian life is a process of growth. It is as we come to Christ, that we are led to a deeper understanding of the meaning of Christian suffering and of Christian fortitude. It is in prayer that we are enabled to grow spiritually and to graduate from the level of being fed by milk as babes to the stage of adulthood and the meat of the Word. Let us bear this in mind as we seek to understand the meaning of prayer.

CONCLUSION:
THE MEANING OF PRAYER

It is when we appreciate the fact that often the answer of God to our prayer is in terms of our spiritual growth, that we begin to understand the true meaning of prayer. Our popular concept of prayer is in terms of expressing our wants and our needs to God. This is certainly an important aspect of prayer; it is petition. Or simply put, "Prayer is asking God for things." But is this the essence of prayer? Is it not the case that prayer has more to do with us seeking to do the will of God than asking Him for things? The example of our Lord in the Garden of Gethsemane is most instructive.

On the night of His betrayal, He went to the garden of Gethsemane. His enemies were pursuing Him. He was deeply conscious that the Cross of Calvary cast its shadow over those closing days of His earthly ministry. Yet, being truly human and Divine, He knew the heavy burden of the Cross. The event is recorded for us by St. Matthew:

"Jesus then came with His disciples to a place called Gethsemane. He said to the, 'Sit here while I go over to pray.' He took with Him Peter and the two sons of Zebedee. Anguish and dismay came over Him. And He said to them, 'My heart is ready to break with grief. Stop here, and stay awake with me.' He went on a little, fell on His face in prayer, and said, 'My Father, if it is possible, let this cup pass from me '. Yet, not as I will, but as Thou wilt" (Matt . 26: 26-39).

As we meditate carefully upon this profoundly moving passage, we are deeply aware of the Humanity of Jesus. As one with mankind, He knew the pains and deep emotional weaknesses of human flesh. And so He expressed His own wish - that the cup of suffering of Calvary should pass. But at the same time He placed highest priority upon the Divine will. So, He could say at the end of this session of deep communion with His Heavenly Father, "My Father, if it is not possible for this cup to pass from me without my drinking it, THY WILL BE DONE!" (Matt. 26: 42 NEB)

"Thy will be done"! My dear friend, is it not precisely in this expression, which calls for OBEDIENCE to the Divine Will, that we find the key to the essential meaning of prayer? For, prayer understood in its most profound significance, is essentially a seeking to know the Will of God rather than seeking to bend the will of God to our own! In prayer, then, we seek not so much to ask God to do things for us as to seek what may be His will for us!

"Thy will be done." It is not without significance that this expression is to be found, not only in the prayer Our Lord gave as a model for prayer to His disciples in all ages, The Lord's Prayer; but also in this prayer in which He communed, in a most intimate and personal manner, with His Heavenly Father.

"THY WILL BE DONE!" In our prayer life, we seek again and again to ask God for the things that we would like. Often we make our plans and in prayer just go to God that He may sanction what we have already decided. This is certainly "putting the cart before the horse." We should, first of all, approach God and seek what His will is for us. Then, we can truly serve Him. For, as we know His will, then we can seek His strength to do what is pleasing in His sight.

Yes, the motto I saw in my aunt's living room is true:

"EVERY PRAYER IS answered in God's way!"

God does answer us in various ways. When we come to Him in prayer as a Loving Father, He often answers us "Yes." But as Sovereign Lord of the universe, sometimes His answer is "No." Again, as the one who is in ultimate control of the affairs of mankind, there are times when His answer is "Wait!" He bids us be patient and not to force the pace of events. But, very often, as our Loving Father His answer is "Grow." He teaches us , in the anvil of experience to grow spiritually even as we seek his will. He assures us "MY GRACE IS SUFFICIENT FOR THEE FOR MY STRENGTH IS MADE PERFECT IN WEAKNESS" (2 Cor. 12:9).

So then, let us come to the throne of Grace confident that God does answer prayer. Let us be persistent in prayer. Let us be trusting in prayer. Let us be faithful in prayer. Most of all, let us be ever seeking to know His will for our lives. Let us pray that we may know His will and have the strength to do the same.

Since every prayer is answered in God's way, then the question naturally comes to mind, "How does one get to know the answer of God?" The answer is at hand - listening!

This writer remembers many years ago a well known Baptist Minister preaching a sermon on prayer in a small church in the Jamaican country side. In it he compared prayer to a telephone conversation. Graphically, he pointed out that a telephone conversation involves both speaking and listening to hear what the other person has to say.

"When we ask a question of another person in a telephone conversation" he declared, "We don't just 'hang up' the phone!" Looking around at the small congregation, he paused and then delivered his statement on prayer, "We wait! We wait for an answer!"

The minister went on to argue that in prayer we should also wait, wait for God's answer to us. He advised the members of his congregation to pause for a few moments at the end of their prayer and to wait for what God has to say to them. The same point was more recently made by a young Methodist Minister preaching to a much larger congregation gathered in worship in Nassau, Bahamas.

Surely, these Ministers of the Gospel have an important lesson for us all to bear in mind as we pursue our prayer life. How many of us regard our prayer as a telephone conversation, one in which we approach God with our own concerns and petitions and in which we, in turn, wait to hear what God has to say to us in response?

Yes, prayer is offering of praise and thanks to God. Prayer is asking God for things. Prayer involves bringing others before the throne of Grace. These are all aspects of prayer in which we are active. But these comprise only one aspect of prayer - the human approach to God.

But what of the other, which is just as important - The Divine response. Surely, if we are to grow at all in our prayer life, then it is essential that we wait, that we wait for what God has in store for us.

LISTENING is essential for our spiritual growth in prayer! We must be prepared to listen, to be sensitive to God's word to us. The old man Eli, when approached by Samuel in the Temple, advised the boy to listen to the Lord and to say, "Speak, Lord, for thy servant heareth!" (1 Sam 3:10).

This too has to be our stance in prayer. Having offered our prayers to God, having made known to him our requests and having sought blessings for others, it is only right that we should wait upon the LORD. This waiting may be both active and passive. It means that we are sensitive to the prompting of the Spirit. Thus, we may learn whether God's answer is positive - "YES", negative, "NO", deliberative, "WAIT" or instructive, "GROW!"

Let us, then, be good listeners. Our prayer life cannot be effective if we are not prepared to listen to God's voice speaking to us, directing us in the way we ought to go. Like Samuel in the Temple we must be willing to listen to what God has to say to us and to act in accord with His answers to us. Our attitude, then, when we have given our praises to God, when we have thanked Him for His blessings, when we have made our petitions, when we have made our confessions and when we have laid our concerns for others before the One on the Throne of Grace should be one of, I am listening, Lord for You, What do you have to say to me?"

Yes, prayer is listening!

MESSAGE FROM THE WAYSIDE PULPIT

"CONTINUE STEADFAST IN PRAYER"

The Wayside Pulpit at Trinity Church, Frederick Street, is one of the most arresting sights in Nassau. Bahamians and tourists alike, in their thousands, pass the busy intersection where the Church is located every day. There on a corner is the Wayside Pulpit, prominently displayed, giving its sage to everyone who passes by.

Known as "The Wayside Pulpit," it preaches a message with a Christian theme day in and day out.

The writer recalls that on several occasions the message has come to him with particular relevance. Early in 1988, for instance, there was the message, which consisted of just four simple words:

CONTINUE STEADFASTLY IN PRAYER

So often in prayer we are inclined to give up. This is especially the case when we face the problem of unanswered prayer or when it is clear that what we are praying for is not in accord with the Will of God. Many people indeed have told of how they became discouraged in prayer and did not continue to be steadfast.

Yet, if our prayer life is to be developed, then we must continue to be steadfast in prayer. It is not enough to just pray "when we feel like it." Nor should we just resort to prayer when we are in trouble. True, in such moments in the course of our journey through life, we are especially close to God and are more than ever in need of prayer.

But prayer does require that we be consistent! We should continue to pray not only when we are in need but when we are in good health, when everything seems to be going our way and all is well. In all the trials and tribulations as well as in the moments of joy and triumph, it behooves us as members of the Body of Christ, to turn to the LORD in prayer that he, by His grace may deliver us and keep us from going the wrong way. Let us ever bear this in mind as we continue our journey through life. Let us constantly turn to him in prayer.

Elijah continued for many days in prayer to God. We sometimes use the expression "prayer warriors." They are the people who continue steadfastly in prayer and are constantly on the move. Let us remember them also in their moments of prayer to the LORD. It is only as we continue steadfastly in prayer that we shall be enabled to win the victory.

8

*P*RAYER *I*S *W*ORK

Hints for Improving Your Prayer Life

"Whenever I am in trouble I pray. And since I'm always in trouble, there is not a day when I don't pray." No "shortcut" to spiritual growth.

We live in an age of rapid communications! Jet-propelled aircraft, moving at supersonic speeds, whisk passengers to their destinations, covering distances in hours, which, in times past, occupied days, and even weeks. Space vehicles, moving at even higher speeds, bolt through the atmosphere, lifting the prospect of interplanetary travel from the realm of science fiction to that of distinct possibility. Telephones and fax messages, working at very high velocities, transmit, in seconds, auditory and visual messages over thousands of miles. And, with the advent and wide usage of computers, it has been found necessary to measure operations in minute fractions of seconds!

All this has resulted in a great demand for things to be done in a hurry. Thus, we have all kinds of "instant substances'" "fast food" establishments and products which can be processed most rapidly.

Now this obsession with speed, while very useful in the technological fields, is not necessarily as desirable or effective in things spiritual! This is especially so in the case of prayer. True, it takes only a few moments for us to offer prayer to God wherever we may be. But the development of our prayer life is not something which can be accomplished "instantly." Rather it requires much effort over a very long period, and it is precisely for this reason that the most devout of the saints "throughout the ages" join in testifying that the cultivation of one's prayer life is a lifetime process!

As we have noted already, the disciples asked Jesus, "LORD, teach us to pray." In so doing they recognized prayer to be an essential component aspect of a person's spiritual development, requiring constant effort and nurture. Prayer, then may be truly described as "a discipline." In plain language, PRAYER CAN BE LEARNED.

It is a learning process which is not to be carried out instantly, but over a long period in a very disciplined manner. Thus, it has been long recognized that hurry is to be avoided in the cultivation of one's prayer life. Today, in our age of speed, we must heed the warning of the saints. "HURRY, IS THE DEATH OF DEVOTION!"

It is essential, then, that we develop our prayer life. For, it is at the heart of our spiritual well being! Thus, we need to be quite intentional and determined in the cultivation of our prayer life.

"A TIME FOR EVERYTHING" "For everything there is a time...." So writes the sage who was inspired to give us the Book of Ecclesiastes. This is indeed very true, and the proper time of doing anything is always crucial. In many situations, it is the major factor which determines the success or failure of a given action.

Now, when it comes to prayer, it is most necessary that we set apart definite times for its practice. And although we are free to offer prayer wherever convenient for us, there are three particular times which seem especially conducive to our prayer life:

Early morning, noon, night.   The Psalmist puts it aptly!
Evening, and morning, and at noon, will I pray, and cry aloud: and
he shall hear my voice" (Psalm 55:17).

First, we should begin the day with prayer! In the Bible, we
note that the great spiritual and administrative leaders began the
day with prayer. Thus Abraham, Moses and Elijah all rose up early
in the morning to pray. And it is recorded of the Master Himself:
"Very early the next morning, long before daylight, Jesus got up
and left the house.

"He went out of the town to a lonely place where he prayed"
(Mark 1:35).

This tradition of praying early in the morning has continued
throughout the ages. The Church Fathers, in their writings, testify
that they found the early morning particularly useful for prayer.
Martin Luther spent hours each day in prayer beginning early in
the morning. John Wesley arose at four every morning to offer
prayer to God. Indeed, the secret of the spiritual power of these
giants of the Christian faith was their prayer life which began early
in the morning. This practice continues today.

I recall a young man telling me about his mother. He recounted that every morning as soon as she opened her eyes, she
turned to God in prayer. "Before she did anything else whatsoever,
even before she put on her slippers, she prayed" he testified.

There can be no better way to begin the day than in prayer!
Indeed, early in the morning, while the day is still fresh, while the
rising sun shines upon the green grass, while our minds are still
uncluttered by the concerns of our mundane responsibilities, it is
good for us to offer prayer to the God of creation. Early in the
morning, as we reflect upon the day before us we can pray for
Divine Guidance in all our deliberations.

Thus, in the morning there are two elements which tend to
predominate - praise and petition. We can begin the day by
offering praise to God as our Creator and as we reflect upon His
Being, and Majesty.

Secondly, it is a time when we make our petitions to God. As we think about the day ahead we may pray for wisdom and strength to meet its challenges. This is why the morning devotional period has been referred to as offering "STRENGTH FOR THE DAY." In our morning prayer we seek spiritual strength to carry us through the day. Yes, it is the best time for the offering of praise and the presenting of our petitions to God.

Then, there is the mid-day prayer. Many of us at this time of day are very busy with our various jobs whether in the office, classroom, in the store or in the workroom. At such a time we may not have a lot of time for prayer.

Still, in the midst of these activities, we can pause to whisper a short prayer, seeking for Divine Blessings and Guidance as we carry out our responsibilities!

Significantly, in some offices, it is very encouraging to note that there is a growing trend - the workers may get together to hold prayer services during lunch break.

There can be no doubt that such "office prayer meetings" are proving to be a major means of spiritual renewal in our community. It is essential to bear in mind, however, that we should never allow our spiritual exercises to interfere with the proper performance of our duties on the job.

Mary Slessor, the famous Scots missionary who served for many years in West Africa, had no patience with the students in her Christian boarding school who had their "prayer time" whenever there were dishes to be washed!

Our mid-day or morning prayers at the office should not, in any way, impede us in our work. Rather, it is to be expected that such prayer will make us more pleasant and efficient workers! Yes, prayer and work should go together.

We come now to consider the evening prayer. The Church has always regarded evening as a special time for prayer. In the Middle Ages, for instance, when the Monastic movement was so influential and extensive, the monks engaged in well prepared corporate prayer in the evening. The evening devotional time was known as "Compline."

Interestingly enough, young people participating in Christian camps in the outdoors, often find evening prayers, around a campfire, very inspiring.

In evening prayer, there are two major elements. First, there is THANKSGIVING, which, as has been seen is very close to PRAISE. As we think about the activities of the day, as we tabulate "the pluses" and the "minuses" we have been through, we can do nothing but thank God for His many blessings so bountifully provided for us. Yes, evening time is a time for thanksgiving!

The other very strong element of evening prayer is CONFES-SION. As we reflect upon the day's activities we may remember moments when we, in some way or the other failed the Master by being unkind, dishonest, and committing acts which were not worthy of those who profess to follow Christ. It is essential that in thinking about them we turn to God and pray for His pardon that we may be redeemed. There is a very beautiful evening prayer which says words to this effect:

And since being human, we could not have passed this day without sinning against Thy Divine Majesty in some way, we pray for thy forgiveness.

How beautiful and how relevant are those words to us. For, ours is a world, a sinful selfish world in need of the forgiving love of God. Thus, we come to the end of the day, thanking God for His goodness and praying for His forgiveness for the sins we have committed. Having then confessed our failings and short comings, we listen to God, and ransomed, healed and forgiven, we can doze off into a restful and refreshing sleep with our conscience clear and being at peace with God, our fellowmen and ourselves!

"A Chapel in Your Home!"

Just as we should have definite times set apart for prayer, it is necessary that we should have places reserved for prayer. Peace

Peace and quiet are essential for development and nurture of our prayer life. As such, we need to have a quiet place where we can be alone with God.

Today, there is much noise around us. Often our homes are crowded and it is not easy to find a place to be alone. With a little imagination and ingenuity, however, you can find a place, in most homes, to be alone with God for the cultivation of the spiritual side of your being.

Yet, as has been emphasized, it is not enough for us to be solitary in our prayer life. In the context of the home, then we should participate in family devotions. Here again, it is necessary to have a special place "set apart" in the home for family devotions. ("Set apart" in Biblical teaching indicates a "holy place", one dedicated to the worship of God!). In the case of the writer's family, this place has inevitably turned out to be the master bedroom, and the time, just before bedtime! Indeed, on occasion, the children have fallen asleep when "Daddy and Mummy" prayed for too long!

While it is ideal to have a place in the home for prayer, there are times when it simply is not convenient to have such a place because of over crowding, sudden responsibilities, etc. Then, the person who wishes to improve his/her prayer life can find a place in the garden, or may go for a morning or evening walk in the neighborhood. Many have found themselves deeply inspired especially during country walks, when they relish the wonders of God's creation. Again, there may be a particular place which brings back memories of some deep spiritual experience. A Minister tells of how it was his practice to return to such a place whenever he was in need of spiritual rejuvenation! Still, for most of us, it is within the home that we must find a place for the cultivation of our souls and the edification of those of our fellow human beings.

In this regard, it is interesting to note that there was a time when very large homes had a "built in chapel." This is hardly ever the case today. When people who have just moved into a new home show us around with pride, they point us to their living room, dining room, bedroom, kitchen, etc. And in some they will ever show you their "built in bar!" Think of it! Whereas in the past, large homes had a chapel, some large homes today have a bar!

Surely, there is a message here for our generation. There can be no doubt that there is a real need for a chapel in a large home. But we don't have to build a large home to have a chapel. Every home, no matter how small or humble can have a chapel, a place where we can meet God as individuals, families or a community group for prayer. There are those, who may be able to build a chapel in their homes, but, for the time being, we can all have a "chapel" in our home, we can all do our best to cultivate our devotional life.

So, whether your home is small or large, you still will need to reserve a place for prayer, a place where you and yours can "enter into the holy of holies," as you enter into deep communion with your Maker.

There is a place of quiet rest, near to the heart of God. A place where sin cannot molest, near to the heart of God.

You need a "chapel in your home," a place where you and yours can dwell continually near to the heart of God.

We must pray methodically then, if we are to develop a disciplined prayer life, we must pray methodically. We need to develop a plan whereby we are consistent in the offering of prayer.

This means that we must not go simply by our emotions. (True there will be times when, because of the challenges and novel situations that we are facing, our prayer will be more intense and frequent than usual). However, we should not just pray when "we feel like it" and neglect our prayer life when we don't! In order to prevent the inertia which may set in by such dependence upon our emotions, we should devise a plan or a timetable of some sort to remind ourselves of our responsibility in the cultivation of our devotional life. Such a plan should not be rigid or inflexible, but should merely be a guide to assist us as we seek to be disciplined in the way we approach Our Maker in prayer. This is very necessary. For, in prayer, as in so many other avenues of endeavors, "PRACTICE MAKES PERFECT."

How, then, should we go about this process of improving our prayer life?

We can begin by careful evaluation of it. Dr. Sangster has reminded us that just as periodically we go to see our physician for a physical "check up," we should "from time to time" undergo a spiritual "check up." Such an exercise can be carried out by honestly asking ourselves hard questions about our own devotional life. Here are some of the types of questions that we should ponder carefully.

How much time am I spending in prayer?

Am I spending enough time in prayer?

Can I afford to spend much more time in prayer than I'm doing now?

Do I offer praise to God as frequently as I should?

Considering the blessings that I have received, do express thanksgiving to God as I should?

Am I helping other members of my family in their prayer life?

Am I honest in offering confession?

Who are some of the people I should be praying for continually?

Are there persons known to me who are in special need of prayer?

Who am I not praying for as I should?

Are there situations in my home, church, nation, world about which I should be praying?

Can I do more to develop my spiritual/prayer life?

Most importantly, is the LORD pleased with my spiritual development?

As you ask yourself these questions, you can begin to take steps to improve in the areas in which you are weak. If the element of praise is lacking, then you should ensure that there is much more time spent in the praise of God. The same method should be used in order to improve the elements of thanksgiving, petition, and confession as you offer prayer to God.

Turning to the prayer of intercession, there can be no doubt that the best way to strengthen it is the compilation of a prayer list. As we have seen, the offering of intercession always adds variety and freshness to our prayer life because there is always so much for us to pray about! We should think of all the persons known to us who are in special need of prayer and list them, either alphabetically or in accordance with their need. Is there any member of our family who is in need? Do we know of anyone in our church or community who is ill? What about that young person preparing for an important examination? And what about that old lady down the street who is so lonely? We should include all such persons in our prayer list. Then we can think about those who belong to our church. We can think about those in authority in the State. We should think about fellow employees at the office, in the factory, in the store or in the field. Are any of them in need of prayer?

We should think about our nation and its leaders. We should think about the world and the problems that are prominent. All these persons and concerns should be included in our prayer list. Indeed, we might soon discover that our prayer list is much longer than we had expected it to be when we began!

Having completed our prayer list, we are now in a position to draw up a timetable. Since we cannot include all the needs and concerns in any one prayer session, we should draw up a timetable in such a way that in the scope of a specified time, say a week, we cover them all.

As has been pointed out, there are three periods during the day which have been found to be especially conducive to the development of our prayer life - early morning, noon and in the evening just before we go to bed. Our prayer life then should be such that we take into account these three major periods and seek to include, in the course of a week, all the major concerns which are on our hearts as we draw near to God in prayer.

It is important to realize that such a prayer timetable is a guide. It can be adapted so that if there are any special concerns we can give them due emphasis in our prayer. In the same way, it is important to bear in mind that the needs and concerns vary from time to time. Therefore, we should revise our prayer time-table periodically so that we may include the new concerns which arise in the course of our earthly sojourn. Thus, our prayer timetable should be changed and/or revised at least once every three months. Of course, we may find it necessary to do so much more frequently, and if need be, we should not hesitate to do so. Our prayer life should not be allowed to become "routine," perfunctory, and stale, but should be "new every morning" as we grow in grace and in our knowledge of God, and in our concern for the welfare of those whom we meet in our experiences.

Below is a suggested timetable, which you may consider as a model in compiling your own prayer timetable:

My Prayer Time Table

"Lord, teach us to pray as John also taught his disciples"

(Luke 11:1).

DAY	MORNING	NOON	EVENING/NIGHT
Sunday			
Monday			
Tuesday			
Wednesday			
Thursday			
Friday			
Saturday			

The above rota can be used as a basis for drawing up a weekly, prayer time table. In the morning the emphasis may be on Adoration, Thanksgiving and Petition. In the evening, the emphasis may be on Thanksgiving and Confession. Prayer of intercession should be included in all prayer times.

Time allotted to prayer will vary according to the temperament, needs and conditions under which we live. However, generally speaking, about 15-20 minutes should be given to morning prayer, 5-10 minutes may be devoted to prayer at the noon and again, 15- 20 minutes should be allocated to evening/ night prayer. Whatever time is devoted to prayer however, it is essential that the elements of sincerity and compassion should be evident as we lift out hearts in prayer to God.

PRAYER OF ADORATION

Prayer of adoration to God, Father, Son and Holy Spirit. Can consist of innovations based on Holy Scripture (especially the Psalms), the verses of a hymn, etc.

PRAYER OF THANKSGIVING

Here we reflect upon the things that we can thank God for - the gift of a new day, life, health, strength, our family and friends, our nation, salvation, etc.

PRAYER OF PETITION

Prayers in which we ask God to help us in our own situation. Here we reflect on our needs - for health, prosperity, for spiritual growth, etc.

PRAYER OF CONFESSION

Here we bring before God our faults and failings, our sins, unwitting and deliberate, and seek Divine Forgiveness. "For we have not a high priest who is unable to sympathize with us in our weaknesses, but one who in every respect has been tempted as we are, yet without sin. Let us then with confidence draw near to the throne of grace, that we may receive mercy and find grace to help in time of need." (Hebrews 4:15-16, RSV).

PRAYER OF INTERCESSION

Here we bring before the throne of grace our concerns for the needs of others.

These include:

PRAYERS FOR THE MEMBERS OF OUR FAMILY

PRAYERS FOR THE CHURCH

Prayers for the members of the congregation we serve (if in pastoral capacity).

Prayers for the Church - its ministry, church growth, evangelism.

Prayers for "young Christians."

PRAYERS FOR THE COMMUNITY

Prayers for persons in authority (The Queen, President, Governor- General, the Prime Minister, the leader of the opposition).

Prayers for Judges and civil servants in executive positions.

Prayer for those who uphold the law, especially the Police, the Military.

Prayers for persons serving in dangerous occupations.

Prayers for couples experiencing problems in their marriage.

Prayer for those taking examination or making crucial decision affecting their own life and the lives of others.

Prayer for those struggling to overcome addictions including alcoholism, drugs, etc.

Prayers for those facing temptation of various kinds.

Prayers for persons involved in caring for the sick.

Prayers for the sick, bereaved and suffering.

PRAYERS FOR THE CHURCH

Prayers for its ministry and members.

Prayers for Christian unity; but ways and means of co-operating within the world wide Methodist community.

Prayers for international agencies such as the United Nations and its ancillary organizations which serve mankind.

RESOURCES FOR IMPROVING YOUR PRAYER LIFE

Since the cultivation of our prayer life is a life long process, it is essential that we should use all the resources that are available to us in doing so. For, we cannot get very far "on our own." Our prayers become repetitive and dull, and eventually sterile if we do not make use of these great spiritual resources of the Church, all of which are readily available to us if only we would use them!

THE BIBLE

First and foremost, the most important resource for developing our prayer life is the Bible. Indeed, Bible study along with prayer are the two main "means of grace" by which our souls are nourished and our spirits revived. Prayer and Bible Study are complimentary and, to be truthful, no devotional exercise is complete if either of these means of grace is lacking!

There are many ways in which the scriptures enrich our prayer life. Sometimes as we read the Bible we are simply just led to offer prayer!

Many of the prayers of the Church are based solidly on scriptures and, indeed some are really paraphrases of scripture passages. Then, we can use the great prayers of the Bible as models to assist in our own prayer life.

Among these we include:

The Prayer of Abraham for the Wicked Cities (Genesis 18:23-33).

The Prayer Offered by Moses for the Israelites.

The Prayer of Dedication of the Temple by Solomon (II Chronicles 6:14-42).

The many prayers to be found in the Book of Psalms (See Chapter 3).

David's great Prayer of Confession (Psalm 51).

Turning to the New Testament, we should think of the prayer life of Jesus: The Prayer of the Great High Priest (Acts 4:23-29).

The opening verses of some of the Epistles of St. Paul.

The prayers of the Book of Revelation.

And, most of all, the Model Prayer, that unique and most meaningful prayer which Our LORD Himself gave in response to the request of His disciples, "LORD, teach us to pray." THE LORD'S PRAYER, or as some scholars prefer to call it, THE DISCIPLES' PRAYER. (Luke 11:2-4 cf Matthew 6:9-13). Also known as "THE FAMILY PRAYER" it is offered by millions of persons, many millions of times every day. It is the model prayer because in it are to be found all the essential elements of prayer including:

1. PRAISE AND ADORATION: "Our Father, which art in heaven, Hallowed by thy name" (vs 9).

2. PETITION: "Thy kingdom come, Thy will be done, on earth as it is in heaven. Give us this day our daily bread... and lead us not into temptation, but deliver us from evil" (vs 10-13).

3. CONFESSION: "And forgive us our debt" (vs 11).

4. INTERCESSION: "As we forgive our debtors" (vs 12).

We note then that this prayer begins in praise, in acknowledging the Fatherhood of God and in the declaration of His Holiness. As we have seen, prayer, which is praise should begin here.

The acknowledgment of the greatness of God, the Divine Father and Creator of all things. Moreover, we have noted already, the Christian can address God as Father by virtue of the redemptive Ministry of Jesus. "See what love the Father has given us, that we should be called the children of God: and so we are! (1 John 3:1 John 1:12-13).

The invocation continues: "Hallowed by thy Name!" Literally this may be rendered, "May thy name be revered as holy because it is holy!" Here we come up against one of the paradoxes of the Christian faith. While we are bid to address God as "Father" in an intimate relationship, we are also to be aware of His holiness, His majesty and His power. In Biblical teaching it is God alone who is holy and everything else derives its holiness from Him. His name is holy because it belongs to and identifies Him. In this invocation, then, we realize that while we are to draw near to God and with millions of Christians dare to call Him Father, we must also be aware of His holiness and have reverence for Him as Creator.

Then there are three petitions in this prayer, and they are quite specific and bold.

First, there is the petition calling for the reign of God to be consummated:

"Thy Kingdom come, Thy Will be done in earth as it is in heaven" (Matt 6:10).

Significantly, the second part of this petition explains the first. The Kingdom of God refers to the reign or rule of God over the whole of His creation. The triumph of the Kingdom of God means that all live according to the will of God. The Christians are to pray fervently for the realization of the reign (rule) of God. In the light of contemporary development in the international political arena, this prayer is especially relevant to our times!

So is the second petition, which is very practical and "down to earth." While, in the long history of the interpretation of this vital text, there have been many who have held to the understanding of bread here in an essentially "spiritualized" manner, it would appear that the consensus of modern scholarship is towards a more mundane interpretation the Master here is calling upon us to pray for the provision of our material needs. This is certainly the emphasis in the contemporary "Materialist" readings of Scripture.

In "the world today" where there are still millions, especially in the poor countries of "the Third World," who are hungry and exist on the brink of starvation, this petition is amazingly relevant!

There are millions belonging to "The Third Church," who when they repeat this petition, are literally praying for the provision of bread to fill their empty bellies and for other necessities of life - shelter, clothing and education for their children. In the light of contemporary human need, it is tantamount to sacrilege to "spiritualize" this important text!

The third petition has always presented difficulties for sensitive Christian souls. They wonder whether it is necessary since they do not think that God would lead them into temptation. However, once we realize that the word "tempt" in Biblical teaching can be used in a two-fold sense, we begin to appreciate its meaning. The word "tempt" can be used in the bad sense of "enticing to do evil" or "provoking to wrath." But it can also be used in a good sense - "to test or to try." It is in the testing experiences of life that our faith grows stronger!

Essentially, then, in this petition we pray that we may not be led to the time of testing of our faith or our witness, but should it be necessary we pray that God will strengthen us to overcome the forces which threaten us. Continually, we note that there is a very strong element of confession. The word used here refers to deliberate sins which we have committed. In this prayer we seek pardon and forgiveness for our past sins. This is followed by and linked to a word of intercession: "As we forgive our debtors."

Here, it is significant to note that our receiving of Divine Forgiveness is inextricably bound up with, if not dependent upon, our willingness to forgive others (Matt. 18:21-35). We who have, in Christ, experienced the joy of forgiveness of God should demonstrate a forgiving attitude to others. The Master then urges us to think of the welfare of others in our prayer life.

Surely, then, this is THE MODEL PRAYER "PAR EXCEL-LENCE." As such it is the prayer which we should not only use as often as we can, but which should also serve as a pattern for us when we "kneel to pray."

This prayer is suitable for all situations and in the midst of the varied experiences of this transitory life, we can use it:

"In all the changing scenes of life, In troubles and in joy."

In situations in which even the most experienced of spiritual giants have found it "difficult to pray," they have turned to it and have discovered it to be an unfailing source of spiritual power.

Still, it is not enough for us simply to repeat "THE LORD'S PRAYER" as often as possible. Rather we should, use it as a model or pattern for us in our prayer life. In our prayers we should include the elements of praise, thanksgiving, confession, petition and intercession, and in so doing our prayer life will be greatly enriched, becoming a source of blessing both for ourselves and for those whom we bring before the Throne of Grace.

The Bible, then is indeed, a very good, most useful and inexhaustible resource for prayer, with nearly every chapter providing the basis for prayer. We should, therefore, always have our Bible "at our side" whenever we pray, especially in our private devotions whether at home, at school, at the office or at Church!

Today, we are coming to realize more and more how important it is to recognize the Bible as a major resource for prayer. The Rev. Dr. Donald E. Collins, for instance, has written a book on the Bible as prayer. It has the arresting title, "LIKE TREES THAT GROW BESIDE A STREAM." In this book the writer expresses the conviction that "the Bible is meant to be prayer as well as read, studied and expounded upon..." This book is highly recommended as a very useful guide for improving your prayer life by means of Bible study. The reader is urged to obtain a copy of this book, which should prove most useful in improving his/her prayer life.

Christians "from all walks of life," throughout the ages, have found another very useful resource in the development of their prayer life - the hymn book! This is not surprising for many of our hymns are really, prayers in song, and as such, there are hymns which contain the various aspects of prayer which we have identified in our study of this vital subject.

Note for instance, that the opening verse of a well known hymn is a prayer of praise:

Immortal, invisible, God only wise,

In light inaccessible hid from our eyes,

Most blessed, most glorious, the Ancient of Days,

Almighty, victorious, Thy great name we praise

Then, a thoughtful prayer of thanksgiving is most intricately, woven into the fabric of this beautiful harvest hymn:

We thank Thee, Lord, for sunshine, dew and rain,

Broadcast from heaven by Thine almighty hand

Source of all life, unnumbered as the sand

Bird, beast, and fish, herb, fruit, and golden grain

Significantly, this unique fishermen's hymn begins with a prayer of petition:

Hear us, O Lord, from heaven, Thy dwelling place:

Like, them of old, in vain we toil all night,

Unless with us Thou go, who art the Light;

Come, then, O Lord, that we may see Thy face

Petition is also the burden of a well known hymn, often used on patriotic occasions:

O God our help in ages past,

Our hope for years to come

Be Thou our guard while troubles last

And our eternal home

Then, confession is at the heart of another well known hymn, which, appropriately, is most often sung in evening services:

Dear Lord and Father of mankind,

Forgive our foolish ways;

Re-clothe us in our rightful mind;

In purer lives Thy service find,

In deeper reverence praise.

There is a hymn which, from start to finish, is a prayer of intercession for the Church:

Jesus, with Thy Church abide;

Be her Saviour, Lord, and Guide,

While on earth her faith is tried;

We beseech Thee, hear us

Finally, one of the most popular of the hymns of the Christian faith, sung at many services, reminds us of the great spiritual resource that is available to us as we pray:

O what peace we often forfeit,

O what needless pain we bear,

All because we do not carry

Everything to God in prayer!

Over the many centuries of the witness of the Church, many books of prayer have been published. The great giants of devotional life in all ages as well as Christians representing all segments of society have contributed to their vast spiritual treasure house. Thus, there are many such prayer books available to us, and others are being produced all the time. Some of these are listed at the end of this book, and no doubt there are many others which you can use in developing your own prayer life.

Here it should be kept in mind that each of us is unique, being so created by our God. So, we should use such prayer books to stimulate us as we continue to strengthen our own devotional life and witness.

The cultivation of one's spiritual life is a very personal thing, especially when it comes to prayer!

JOINING/FORMING A PRAYER GROUP

There can be no doubt that there is much to be gained spiritually by participating in prayer along with others. As has been repeated on several occasions, we are, by nature, gregarious. We love the company of fellow human beings. "It is not good for man to be alone."

This is, indeed, very true of our prayer life. We are greatly strengthened in its development as we share with others the spiritual insights which have come to us in our own prayer experience. It is, therefore, most advantageous and advisable for us to seek to have prayer often with others.

The old custom of "having family prayer," which appeared to be in decline for some years, is now making a comeback. It is encouraging to note that many Christians speak with pride of the fact that they have regular family prayers. This is a very good trend and should be encouraged.

Those of you who are parents especially, are urged to have family prayers as often as possible. If you have small children, then remember to pray with them (and for them) every morning and at bedtime. (Children are very receptive to prayer and, some have very inquiring minds. Indeed, sometimes they come up with questions about prayer which we find hard to answer! Let us continually offer prayer to God with our children!) Significantly, many leading Christians today will readily testify that they are strong in the faith today primarily because their parents began to teach them to pray while they were still little children.

The family that prays together stays together.

ATTENDING PRAYER MEETINGS

Then, of course, there are the prayer meetings in our churches. Again, it is encouraging to note that there is a revival in this aspect of the life of the church. In many churches, the week night prayer meeting is well attended and a source of spiritual power for the whole church.

Here it is suggested that we attend prayer meeting at least one week night per week! It is not enough for us to go to Church on Sunday. We should set apart at least one night per week when we offer prayer as part of a worshipping congregation.

JOINING A PRAYER GROUP OR STARTING ONE IN YOUR HOME! One of the most significant features of contemporary Christianity is the growth of "the prayer cell movement" in the homes of members! In many neighborhoods in countries "all over the world," special prayer groups are springing up. Some of these are small and some are large. Some have prayers for an hour or two while there are others which, in some cases, last through the night.

Indeed, we are hearing more and more about "all night prayer meetings" or "round the clock prayer meetings." Significantly, it has been the experience of many devout Christians that their own prayer life has been greatly enriched by being in the company of fellow believers. The spiritual depth and the length of time devoted to prayer have both been enhanced by participation in prayer groups, sharing with others in an act of communion with God. Those who can barely pray for a few minutes "on their own" testify that as part of a prayer group, or "prayer band," they can continue for hours non-stop! Yes, our prayer life is greatly enriched in the company of others. In prayer, as in so many other avenues of human endeavor, "iron sharpeneth iron." Thus, if you would like to improve in this area, then you should consider joining a prayer group or cell which meets in your neighborhood.

Suppose, however, you inquire and you find that there is not such a prayer group meeting in your neighborhood! What should you do? The answer is at hand - start one! You should give most serious consideration to beginning a prayer group in the neighborhood in which you reside, or in the office where you work. To take the initiative in such a situation may be easier than you think! For, if you inquire, you may very well find that there are others, like yourself, who are anxious, just dying, to share in a prayer group of some kind. People today are faced with so many anxieties, so many problems, so many trials and tribulations, and so much loneliness in the midst of crowd, that many are only too glad to participate in a prayer cell. Now, there are several ways in which you can go about this! Perhaps, the most effective way is for you to invite several persons in your neighborhood to your home for prayer. Or you can discuss with them the need for prayer in the light of the problems of the community. Still, another approach may be to begin by discussing with them some needs of the neighborhood greater security, the need for a "clean up" project, or the need for better they, etc.

It may well be that as you discuss these needs, you may be led to join with your neighbors in prayer about them. And not only prayer; you may be led to take action to improve the conditions of your community. Thus, your prayers may result in the transformation of your neighborhood, making it a better place for you and your neighbors to live in. Indeed, the offering of prayer together may lead to work for the improvement of the community. Prayer and work are inextricably bound up with each other!

It is essential, then, that we should work at our prayer life. Prayer is at once simple and most profound. Prayer can be learned. Concisely, "PRAYER IS WORK!" Such being the case, let us seek continually to improve our own prayer life. And when we meet our neighbors, and friends and foes alike, let us invite them to share with us in prayer. Yes, let us challenge them with these arresting words:

Come Let Us Pray!

NOTES

CHAPTER 1
WHAT IS PRAYER?
1. Definitions of prayer given at a seminar on prayer held at St. Michael's Methodist Church, Boyd Sub-division, Nassau, Bahamas, sometime early in 1990. **2.** Metropolitan Anthony, Living Prayer (Springfield, Illinois: Templegate, Publishers, 1966, P.95. Metropolitan Anthony (who is also known to many persons as Anthony Bloom) is a Bishop of the Russian Orthodox Church in Great Britain. He is very well known for his preaching and works on the spiritual life and is often called upon to comment on religious and spiritual affairs. He appears regularly in religious broadcasts on Radio and television. **3.** Second verse of the hymn "Lord, teach us now to pray aright" by James Montgomery 1771 - 1854.

CHAPTER 2
PRAYER IS PRAISE
1. Popular Gospel song written by the well known singer, and composer Andre Crouch. 2. St. Augustine of Hippo (354 - 430), recognized as one of the great Christian thinkers of all time, expressed the meaning of human existence in these immortal words, which are to be found at the beginning of his "Confessions."

CHAPTER 3
PRAYER IS THANKSGIVING
1. Opening verse of a hymn of praise written by the German Hymnologist Joachim Neander, 1650 - 80, translated by Catherine Winkworth, 1829 - 78 others.

CHAPTER 4
PRAYER IS PETITION
1. Second Stanza of the hymn, "Come, my soul thy suit prepare", by John Newton, 1725 - 1807. **2.** Collins Dictionary L - Z, ed. D. Halsey (London: MacMillan, 1977), P. 753. **3.** William Shakespeare. **4.** Verse from the very well known hymn, "What a Friend we have in Jesus", written by Joseph Medlicott Scriven, 1820 - 86.

CHAPTER 5
PRAYER IS CONFESSION
1. The writer has dealt with the nature of David's sins elsewhere. See J. Emmette Weir. **2.** See Dennis J. McCarthy, Treaty and Covenant: Analecta Biblica (Rome: Pontifical Biblical Institute, 1963). **3.** Scholars have clearly demonstrated that the maintenance of justice in the sacral community was the major domestic

responsibility of the king. The matter is dealt with carefully by John Gray in his illuminating, The Biblical Doctrine of the Reign of God (Edinburgh: T. & T. Clark, 1979) and by Witlam in The Just King (Sheffield: JSOT, 1980). See also A.R. Johnson, Sacral Kingship in Anchient Israel (Cardiff: University Press, 1967). **4.** See James Limburg, (The Prophets and the Powerless (Atlanta: John Knox Press, 1977). **5.** On this subject see the excellent, comphresensive study by N.H. Whybray (London: Student Christian Movement Press, 1967). **6.** The significance of prayer as therapeutic process was discussed by Dr. Patrick Roberts in a very perceptive and illuminating address at a Prayer Seminar at Wesley Methodist Church, Nassau, Bahamas, in July, 1991. **7.** Those who would like to pursue exhaustive study of this Psalm may consult the various commentaries, notably the major work by Author Weiser, The Psalms) **8.** The writer was an Episcopal priest who had a deep social concern which was demonstrated throughout his ministry in a Parish in New York.

CHAPTER 6
PRAYER IS INTERCESSION
1. See Matthew 12:22; Mark 6:34-44; Luke 18:35-43; John 11. **2.** On compassion see J. Emmette Weir, The Challenge of Compassion (Nassau Bahamas, 1978). **3.** The late Paul Tillich, the famous German-American theologian claimed that the major fear of contemporary man is the fear of "meaninglessness." **4.** William Shakespeare, The Merchant of Venice. **5.** In many years of hospital visitation in a number of countries including the United States, the United Kingdom, Jamaica and The Bahamas, the writer has very seldom come across any one who refused a word of prayer. Indeed, in most cases, they positively welcomed a word of prayer and often requested prayer, especially when very ill! **6.** With the rapid spread of the disease AIDS, it is essential that Christians should include concerns for those that Christians should include concerns for those suffering from this disease in their prayers of intercession. Pastors should be especially sensitive to the needs of persons suffering from AIDS and include special prayers for them in preparing orders of Service.

CHAPTER 7
PRAYER IS LISTENING!
1. This account of the healing of her son is recorded by his mother Kweda Sinclair in "The Methodist Messenger" Nassau, Bahamas 1989, P.10. It is a dramatic, inspiring story demonstrating that the healing power of God is still available to us today, and should prove a source of comfort and encouragement to many who are suffering now. **2.** On the life of Thomas Coke, see John Poxon, Thomas Coke, (Kingston, Jamaica, 1989). **3.** This well known meditation, known as "The Prayer of Serenity" has been a source of inspiration to many throughout the ages. 4. Sermon preached

by the late Rev. A.E. Brown at a Baptist church in the Parish of Portland, Jamaica sometime in 1956. 5. Sermon preached by the Rev. Dr. Colin Archer at Ebenezer Methodist Church, Nassau, Bahamas on Sunday July 28, 1991.

CHAPTER 8
PRAYER IS WORK!

1. The late Isaac Bashevis Singer was a distinguished American Jewish writer and poet. He had already made a considerable contribution in literary pursuits in his native Poland, when he migrated to the United States, where he gradually earned recognition as an interesting and provocative writer publishing works in both Yiddish and English. **2.** Donald Collins, The Trees That Grow Beside a Stream (Nashville: Abingdon Press, 1991). **3.** Opening Stanza of the well known hymn by William Chalmers Smith 1824 - 1908. **4.** These verses are extracted from a harvest hymn which comes to us from the Isle of Man, located off the coast of England, Great Britain. Written by William Henry Gill, (1839 - 1923), it vividly describes the simple rustic life style of a hard working people who eked out a living by means of peasant farming and fishing. This hymn, marked by a deep abiding faith in the Providence of God, "The Bountiful Provider," has proved to be popular at harvest services in churches in the Caribbean, where socio-economic conditions of many rural communities, are very similar to those reflected in the hymn. **5.** Opening stanza of the well known hymn by the famous hymn writer, Isaac Watts, 1674-1748. **6.** Opening stanza of hymn by the well known American poet, John Greenleaf Whittier, 1807-92. **7.** Opening stanza of hymn written by Theomad Benson Pollock, 1836- 96. **8.** Extract from the opening verse of the hymn which is a favorite of many Christians, which has proved a great source of consolation in times of bereavement, "What a Friend we have in Jesus." **9.** See Appendix. **10.** There can be no doubt that prayer, like so ,many other spheres of endeavour, is greatly enriched by sharing with others. Indeed, while there are those who are able to spend many hours in prayer in solitude which is often necessary in the cultivation of the spiritual life, most confess that in the company of others, in joining incorporate prayer, their own spiritual development is greatly facilitated. This is not surprising, considering the essentially gregarious nature of man. As one Christian leader john Donne puts it, "No man is an Island." Or, in the profound words of holy Scripture, "It is not good for man to be alone." Gen.2:18

APPENDIX
Additional Resources for Growth in Prayer

The process of growth in prayer is a life long experience! Thus we should be seeking, constantly and consistently, to grow in this aspect of our spiritual development. This book, therefore (originally prepared especially for the observance of the Bahamas National Year Of Call To Prayer, marking 500 years of christian witness in the western hemisphere!) is just a beginning!

The reader is encouraged to continue to develop his/her prayer life by making use of the many resources which are available. For, throughout the ages there have been those who have felt the call and calm of God upon them to devote their gifts, time and energies to the development of their prayer life, and so have rightly contributed to the spiritual treasure of the church. Below, some of these resources are listed here. Do make use of, if not all, some of them!

1. MAJOR WORKS ON PRAYER

The various denominations all have their own prayer books and devotional resources and the reader may consult his/her spiritual leader for the relevant works. Many books and other resources on prayer (Such as audio & video, tapes, films, cards, rosaries, etc.) Are produced by the churches. Organizations such as "The Upper Room" of Nashville, Tennessee, The International Bible Reading Association, Robert Denholm House, Surrey, England: The International Bible Societies and the Scripture Union of Great Britain publish very good material on prayer.

2. BOOKS ON PRAYER

A CHAIN OF PRAYER THROUGHOUT THE AGES. This is a classic work which has brought great inspiration and spiritual strengthen many persons "From All Walks of Life."

METROPOLITAN, ANTHONY. (Anthony Bloom). Living Prayer, Springfield, Illinois: Templegate Publishers.

_____, Beginning To Pray. New York: Paulist Press

Albans, Helen. PRAYING WITH STICKY FINGERS. London: Methodist Publishing House. Lesson on how to pray with small children.

Allen, Charles. GOD'S PSYCHIATRY. Nashville: Broadman Press.

Baillie, John. A DIARY OF PRIVATE PRAYER. Edinburgh: St. Andrew Press

Barclay, William. PRAYERS FOR THE PLAIN MAN. London: SCM Press.

_____, PRAYERS FOR HEALTH AND HEALING. London: SCM Press

Boyd, Malcolm. ARE YOU RUNNING WITH ME JESUS? New York: Holt, Rinehart & Winston.

Champlin, Joseph BEHIND CLOSED DOORS: A HANDBOOK ON HOW TO PRAY. New York: Paulist Press.

Collins, Donald. THE TREES THAT GROW BESIDE A STEAM. Nashville: Abingdon press.

Community of Taize. PRAYING TOGETHER IN WORD AND SONG. Oxford: A.R. Mowbray.

Copeland, Kenneth. PRAYER: YOUR FOUNDATION FOR SUCCESS. Fort Worth, TX: KCP Publications

Coupland, Susan. BEGINNING TO PRAY IN OLD AGE. Cambridge, MA.: Cowley Press.

Davidson, Graema J. ANYONE CAN PRAY: A GUIDE TO METHODS OF CHRISTIAN PRAYER. New York: Paulist Press.

Davis, Elisabeth. FOR EACH DAY A PRAYER. New York: Dodge Publishing Co.

Eadie, Donald. PRAYING NOW. Peterborough: Methodist Publishing House.

Ellis, Neil. THE POWER OF THE BLOOD. Nassau, Bahamas.

Green, Thomas H. WHEN THE WELL RUNS DRY. Notre Dame, Indiana: Ave Maria Press.

Gribble, Robert F. OUR STEWARDSHIP OF PRAYER. Published by the Stewardship Department, Prebysterian Church of the US.

George, A. Raymond. COMMUNION WITH GOD IN THE NEW TESTAMENT. Peterborough: Methodist Publishing House.

Hassell, David J. HEALING THE ACHE OF ALIENATION: PRAYING THROUGH AND BEYOND BITTERNESS. New York: The Paulist Press.

Higgins, John J. MERTON'S THEOLOGY OF PRAYER. Spencer, MA.: Cistercian Publications.

Irwin, Kevin. LITURGY, PRAYER & SPIRITUALITY. New York: Paulist press.

Jenkins, Daniel Thomas. PRAYER AND THE SERVICE OF GOD. New York: Morehouse Gorham Co.

Kallinger, John. BREAD FOR THE WILDERNESS, WINE FOR THE JOURNEY: THE MIRACLE OF PRAYER AND MEDITATION. Waco, TX: Word Books

Merton, Thomas. CONTEMPLATIVE PRAYER. New York: Herder & Herder.

Mensies, L. (Editor). LIFE AS PRAYER AND OTHER WRITING OF EVELYN UNDERHILL. Harrisburg, PA: Morehouse Publishing Co.

Murray, Andrew. WITH CHRIST IN THE SCHOOL OF PRAYER. Springdale, PA: Whitaker House

Pickard, Jan S. & Edwards, Maureen. OCEANS OF PRAYER: AN ANTHOLOGY OF PRAYERS & MEDITATIONS FROM THE WORLD CHURCH. Peterborough: Methodist Publishing House.

Peterson, Eugene H. ANSWERING GOD: THE PSALMS AS TOOLS FOR PRAYER. San Francisco: Harper & Row.

Price, Fredrick. HOW TO OBTAIN STRONG FAITH. Tulsa, OK: Harrison House.

Quoist, Michael. PRAYERS FOR CHRISTIAN LIVING. London: SCM Press.

CONTEMPORARY PRAYERS, RELEVANT AND DOWN TO EARTH. Especially appropriate for youth services, meetings, devotions at camps, etc.

Torry, R.A. HOW TO OBTAIN FULLNESS OF POWER. Springdale, PA: Whitaker House.

Sangster, William. LORD TEACH US TO PRAY. Springdale, PA: Whitaker House. See Chapter Four "The Power of Prayer."

Whitney, Doris E. TO BE HONEST, LORD. Peterborough: Methodist Publishing House.

Wright, John H. A THEOLOGY OF PRAYER. Pueblo Press

ABOUT THE AUTHOR

Dr. Joseph Emmette Augustus Weir is a Methodist minister. A native of the Bahamas Islands. He studied at the United Theological College of the West Indies, Kingston, Jamaica. He has earned a Bachelor of Divinity from London University, Master of Sacred Theology from Christian Theological Seminary, and Doctor of Philosophy from University of Aberdeen. He is presently a member of the faculty of Templetton Theological Seminary. He has served in pastorates in Jamaica, Eleuthera and New Providence.

OTHER BOOKS FROM Pneuma Life Publishng

Beyond the Rivers of Ethiopia $6.95
Beyond the Rivers of Ethiopia is a powerful and revealing look into God's purpose for the Black Race. It gives scholastic yet simple answers to questions you have always had about the Black presence in the Bible.At the heart of this book is a challenge and call to the offspring of the Children of Africa both on the continent and throughout the world to come to grips with their true identity as they go Beyond the Rivers of Ethiopia.

Strategies for Saving the Next Generation $4.95
by Dave Burrows
This book will teach you how to start and effectively operate a vibrant youth ministry. This book is filled with practical tips and insight gained over a number of years working with young people from the street to the parks to the church. Dave Burrows offers the reader vital information that will produce results if carefully considered and adapted. Excellent for Pastors and Youth Pastor as well as youth workers and those involved with youth ministry.

Talk to Me $5.95
by Dave Burrows
A guide for dialogue between parents and teens. This book focused on the life issues that face teens, ranging from drugs to sex to parents to music to peer pressure. This book will help both teenagers and parents gain a new understanding on these age old issues. Written "in your face" by a man who knows what it is to be a troubled youth living in a world of violence, drugs and street culture.

BOOKS BY Dr. Myles Munroe:

Becoming A Leader	**$9.95**
Becoming A Leader Workbook	**$7.95**
How to Transform Your Ideas into Reality	**$7.95**
Single, Married, Separated and Life After Divorce	**$7.95**
Understanding Your Potential	**$7.95**
Understanding Your Potential Workbook	**$6.00**
Releasing Your Potential	**$7.95**
The Pursuit of Purpose	**$7.95**

Mobilizing Human Resources $7.95
by Pastor Richard Pinder

Pastor Pinder gives an in-depth look at how to organize, motivate and deploy members of the body of Christ in a manner that produces maximum effect for your ministry. This book will assist you in organizing and motivating your 'troops' for effective and efficient ministry. It will also help the individual believer in recognizing their place in the body, using their God given abilities and talents to maximum effect.

The Minister's Topical Bible $14.95
by Derwin Stewart   **Leather Bound $19.95**

The Minister's Topical Bible covers every aspect of the ministry providing quick and easy access to scriptures in a variety of ministry related topics. This handy reference tool can be effectively used in leadership training, counseling, teaching, sermon preparation and personal study.

Four Laws of Productivity $7.95
by Dr. Mensa Otabil

In Genesis 1:28, God commanded man to do four things: (1) "Be fruitful, and (2) multiply, and (3) replenish the earth, and (4) subdue it: and have dominion .." In the past, many people read and thought that this scripture only meant to have many children. This scriptural passage is not confined to reproduction, but is the foundation for all productivity. The Four Laws of Productivity by Dr. Mensa Otabil will show you how to: Discover God's gift in you, develop the gift, and how to be truly productive in life. The principles revealed in this timely book will radically change your life.

Available at your Local Bookstore
or by contacting:

Pneuma Life Publishing
P.O. Box 10612
Bakersfield, CA 93389

TO ORDER CALL TOLL FREE
1-800-727-3218